John Knox:
The Scottish Reformer

rewritten by

Dorothy Martin

MOODY PRESS
CHICAGO

© 1982 by
THE MOODY BIBLE INSTITUTE
OF CHICAGO

Original title: *John Knox and the Scottish Reformation* by G. Barnett Smith (London: Partridge, n.d.).

Library of Congress Cataloging in Publication Data

Martin, Dorothy.
  John Knox, the Scottish reformer.

  Adapted from: John Knox and the Scottish Reformation / by G. Barnett Smith.
  1. Knox, John, 1505-1572. 2. Reformation—Scotland—Biography. 3. Scotland—Church history—16th century. I. Smith, George Barnett, 1841-1909. John Knox and the Scottish Reformation. II. Title.
BX9223.M37   1982   285'.2'0924 [B]   82-12608
ISBN 0-8024-4354-0

       1 2 3 4 5 Printing/LC/Year 87 86 85 84 83 82

Printed in the United States of America

PREFACE

John Knox lived during the most stirring times in Scotland's history. The wave of Protestant enthusiasm had swept over many parts of Europe and reached Scotland while he was still a boy. Just as the clergy abroad had lost the respect of the people through their excesses, so the clergy of Scotland by their arbitrary and immoral conduct precipitated the revolution in which Knox played so vital a role.

By 1525, Lutheran books were so widely read in Scotland that Parliament banned them. Nevertheless, the number of Protestants multiplied in spite of the fierce fires of persecution. Patrick Hamilton, the first martyr in Scotland for the cause of the Reformation, was condemned to the flames at Saint Andrews in 1528, when he was only twenty-three. Persecution raged from

1530 to 1546, but the death of the martyrs only hastened the triumph of the new doctrines. Many of the nobles, jealous of the wealth, influence, and arrogance of the Roman Catholic clergy, threw in their lots with the common people.

Then John Knox arose, a man whose firm, uncompromising stand for truth in spite of opposition has had few rivals in history. His influence over his nation and over individuals was unexampled. God raised him up for the work that had to be done, and that no other man could have accomplished. This great apostle of the Scottish Reformation laid the basis for a national faith to which his countrymen responded. He is justly entitled to rank with those whose names shall continue to live forever.

EUROPE

Scotland

Glasgow

Dundee

Edinburgh

England

London

Dieppe

East Germany

Frankfurt

France

Switzerland

Geneva

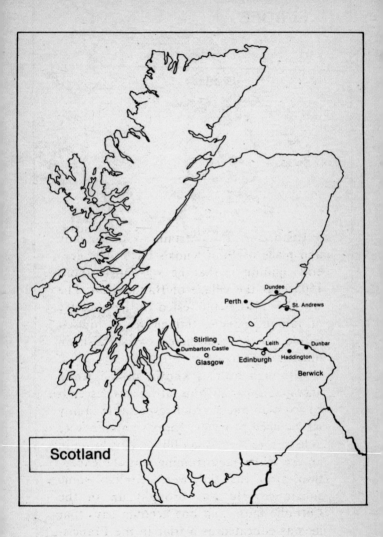

Scotland

1

Historians are uncertain about the date and place of John Knox's birth. The general opinion is that he was born about 1505 near the village of Haddington. The world is always interested in the ancestry of famous people, though Knox himself would not have bothered to establish an illustrious pedigree.

Although little is known of the Knox ancestry, apparently his father was descended from an ancient and respectable family who owned property. Knox's parents were able to give their son a liberal education in an era when such training was the exception, proof that they were people of some substance. He was brought up in the Catholic faith, and one account says that he was educated as a friar in the Franciscan monastery of Haddington.

After Knox had mastered the Latin language, he was sent to the University of Glasgow in the winter of 1521-1522, when he was seventeen. In the early part of the sixteenth century, the curriculum in Scottish universities centered in Aristotelian philosophy, scholastic theology, and common law. The teachers were trained in Europe, as was John Major, the famous scholar of that generation under whom Knox studied at the University of Glasgow. Knox, like all of his educated contemporaries, learned to speak and write Latin fluently. Much later in life he taught himself Greek and Hebrew.

In the university Knox delighted in learning from Major the art of logical argument. All of Knox's writings show his skill in using logic to investigate truth. But he was impatient with the uselessness of much that was taught in the university, and he left without taking the degree of Master of Arts. He studied theology on his own and for a time taught philosophy in one of the classes at the university, becoming known for his skill in dialectics.

About 1529 he was ordained as a priest, before the age fixed by the canons of the church. Then, as he read Jerome's and Augustine's writings, he gradually abandoned the study of scholastic theology and threw off many of the superstitions of the Roman Catholic church. He did not yet formally declare himself a Protestant, however. From 1540 to 1543 he acted as a notary in Haddington and there gave up his orders in the church of Rome.

By this time those of the Reformed persuasion included many members of noble Scottish families who were alienated from Catholicism by the corruption they saw in its doctrines and practices. As the Reformers increased in numbers, they began to advocate their beliefs boldly and openly attacked the Roman Catholic church. In spite of the bishops' attempts to check the growing movement by harsh legislation, the people continued to read the psalms and epistles in their own language. Even though Knox still did not take a public stand in favor of the Reformed doctrines, he was delighted with the evidences of religious interest.

Other influences worked to bring Knox to the place of boldly stating his belief in Protestant doctrine. The Scottish Parliament passed an act in 1542 declaring it lawful for people to read the Scriptures in the Scottish language rather than in Latin. This was an important step, and soon the Bible was on every gentleman's table, and the New Testament in almost everyone's hand. As Knox became increasingly vocal in his support of Protestant doctrines, the clergy feared his influence on others. Cardinal Beaton, the enemy of all religious reform, hired assassins to kill him. God intervened and brought him under the protection of two influential families who hired him to tutor their sons.

At this time George Wishart became the most important influence in Knox's life. Wishart had traveled in Germany and England, and when he returned to Scotland, he was eager to bring a knowledge of the Lutheran faith to his countrymen. His earnest preaching of the Reformed doctrines in Scotland was responsible for building up the new faith.

After meeting Wishart, Knox never wavered in his desire to establish in Scotland "the only true conception of the primitive Church, as based on the teaching of Christ and the Apostles." He was now clearly conscious of his great mission and impetuously joined Wishart. He carried a two-handed sword as a protection for Wishart when he preached. But Wishart, knowing he would be arrested by Cardinal Beaton, urged Knox to "return to your pupils. One is sufficient for sacrifice." Wishart was martyred in Saint Andrews in March 1546.

Two months later Cardinal Beaton was murdered, and suspicion fell on Knox, who was known to be the cardinal's enemy. Though he had no part in the cardinal's assassination, Knox believed that the laws of God and of society allowed tyrants to be put away when all efforts to correct their abuses failed.

The cardinal's murderers fled to the castle of Saint Andrews, and Knox was compelled for his own safety to join them at Easter, 1547. His zeal and theological gifts were so evident that the leaders of the Reformed party formally called him to the ministry.

One of the leaders was the eloquent preacher John Rough, who gave the charge to Knox. "In the name of God, and of His Son, Jesus Christ, and in the name of all that presently call you by my mouth, I charge you that you refuse not this holy vocation, but . . . that you take the public office and charge of preaching, even as you look to avoid God's heavy displeasure, and desire that He shall multiply His graces unto you."

Then, addressing the congregation, Rough asked, "Was this not your charge unto me? And do ye not approve this vocation?" They all answered, "It was, and we approve it."

Knox, overwhelmed by this unexpected and solemn charge, was unable to address the audience, but burst into tears, rushed out of the assembly, and shut himself in his room. He was unsure of his ability to fulfill the responsibility of the charge. In spite of his apparently bold character, he showed this diffidence several times in taking positions to which he was called.

But, having accepted the ministerial office, he was well received in both the castle and the parish church of Saint Andrews. Knox did not believe that ordination by man was a necessary part of Christ's command to preach, nor did he think it necessary for the presbyters to lay hands on him to qualify him to preach. Convinced that God had called him to the ministry, he did not need man's approval.

He boldly preached that the pope was anti-Christ and that the Roman Catholic church system was completely false and anti-scriptural. His courage brought victory to the Protestant cause in Saint Andrews. Those in the castle who heard him preach, as well as the people in the town, renounced Catholicism and took the Lord's Supper as Protestants.

Unfortunately, because of friendship with Scottish royalty, the French court sent a fleet in July 1547 to lay siege to the castle of Saint Andrews. No one could rescue the protesters who had taken refuge there after the cardinal's murder. They bravely resisted but were finally overcome. Knox was taken prisoner along with the others, though that was contrary to the terms of the surrender. The prisoners were taken to Rouen and confined to the galleys as slaves. In addition to the hardships of captivity, they were loaded with chains and forced to row the ships under the whips of the overseers.

Even worse, the prisoners had to endure the indignities that Catholics at that time inflicted on Protestants within their power. Those included attempts to force the prisoners to change their religion. Throughout the rest of the hot summer and the long winter that followed, the captors used cajoling, threats, and beatings to induce the prisoners to accept the Catholic faith. But not one was willing even to pretend compliance in order to escape torture.

One day a painted image of the Virgin Mary was brought onto one of the galleys, and a prisoner was ordered to kiss it. Instead, he threw it into the river, exclaiming, "Let the Lady save herself. She is light enough; let her swim." Impressed by such boldness, the officers then left the prisoners to their own beliefs.

In the summer of 1548, the galleys returned to Scotland, lying along the east coast, watching for English ships. While the ship lay on the coast between Dundee and Saint Andrews, someone asked Knox if he recognized the spires of Saint Andrews.

The sickly and emaciated captive replied, "I know it well. I see the steeple of that place where God first opened my mouth in public to His glory; and I am fully persuaded, how weak soever I now appear, that I shall not depart this life, till that my tongue shall glorify His godly name in that same place."

In spite of Knox's poor health resulting from the long imprisonment, he constantly cheered his fellow prisoners with hopes of escape and release. Some of Knox's fellow prisoners who were confined in Mont Saint Michel asked him whether it was lawful for them to try to escape from prison. They were afraid the attempt might bring greater hardship to those left behind. Knox replied, "You are at liberty to try as long as no blood is shed." Encouraged by this, the men made a successful escape without harm to anyone.

But even Knox's buoyant spirits sometimes gave way to despondency. His strong emotions alternated from exaltation to depression. Between bouts of fever during his captivity, he composed a confession of his faith, based upon his teaching at Saint Andrews. He found a way to send the confession to his friends in Scotland in order to strengthen them in the faith.

Knox was freed in February 1549 on the express intercession of Edward VI, king of England, after an imprisonment of nearly two years. His hard experiences while a captive seriously affected his health for the remainder of his life. He never forgot the breach of faith by the French in taking him captive, nor the ignominy to which

they subjected him. He had a lifelong con-
viction that no good thing could come of
French policy or of the French religion.

2

Though free from slavery on the galley, Knox was not free to return to his native land, for conditions in Scotland made it unsafe for him to do so. Therefore, he went to England, rejoicing in the encouraging change in its religious climate since the accession to the throne of Edward VI, the young Protestant king. Knox soon became influential with Archbishop Cranmer and others at the English court.

King Edward's council employed a number of popular, orthodox preachers in various parts of the kingdom to teach the principles of the Reformation to lay people, to illiterate clergy, and to those disenchanted with the Roman church. Soon after Knox's arrival in London, knowing his reputation as a preacher and his sufferings for the faith, the council sent him to preach in Berwick.

Knox's earnestness brought numbers of people from Catholicism. One of the most obvious results of his preaching was the change in morals of the soldiers in the garrison. However, the bishop of Durham was greatly disturbed by the Protestant teachings because of his strong leaning to the tenets of the Roman church. The bishop accused Knox of teaching that the mass was idolatrous and set a day for Knox to appear and either defend his belief or abandon it. Knox, whose motto in controversy was "spare no arrows," completely silenced the bishop. Instead of stopping Knox, the bishop's actions had caused his fame to spread more widely throughout the north of England.

The Privy Council showed its approval of Knox's ministry by appointing him one of King Edward's chaplains in 1551. Archbishop Cranmer consulted him about the revision of the *Book of Common Prayer,* and particularly about Knox's forty-five Articles of Religion. Knox did not get all of the reforms he wanted, but he was able to push through an important change in the article dealing with Communion. He influenced the Church of England to support the Genevan doctrine of the Eucharist, which held that the body and blood of the Lord Jesus was present in the elements *only* in a spiritual sense. After Mary became queen, Catholic churchmen complained about the change, regretting that "one man had had so much authority."

Knox not only had the Roman Catholics as open enemies, but also had covert ones like the duke of Northumberland, who was infuriated by Knox's plain speaking on all questions. He tried to curb Knox's influence as one of the king's chaplains by offering him a bishopric. Knowing the offer's purpose, Knox unhesitatingly rejected it.

Whenever Knox preached at court, his sermons pleased the king, who also was eager, for a different reason, to promote him within the church. However, as Knox saw what went on in the king's court, anxiety gripped him. He had not the slightest doubt of the piety and sincerity of the young king. All who knew Edward VI praised him. But he was surrounded by advisors who were indifferent to religion and who would change faiths whenever a change of rulers made it expedient to do so. Edward's nobles were interested only in their wealth and the security of their own positions.

God's faithful servants—Latimer, Knox, Bradford, and others—courageously seized every opportunity to censure the ambition, greed, oppression, and lack of religion so evident in the court. That is clear from Knox's last sermon before King Edward. His text was John 13:18, "He that eateth bread with me hath lifted up his heel against me." He pointed out that godly, noble kings were often surrounded by false, ungodly officers and counselors. He illustrated the message with the scriptural examples of Ahithophel under King David, Shebuel under Hezekiah, and Judas under Jesus Christ.

"What wonder is it then," he demanded, "if a young and innocent king be deceived by crafty, covetous, wicked, and ungodly counsellors?"

King Edward, never strong, gradually weakened, and it was obvious that he would not live long. To the unspeakable grief of Protestant England and Europe, King Edward died in July, 1553. Knox had long dreaded the event and greeted it with keen anguish. He warned the people, who hailed Queen Mary's coronation with delight, that calamities lay ahead for the nation.

Knox left London the day Mary was proclaimed queen and went to live in the north of England, waiting apprehensively for announcement of the new government's policies. When Mary issued a proclamation declaring that no Protestant would be persecuted, he returned south and resumed his teaching and preaching. He continually prayed for Queen Mary by name and for the suppression of any who might plot rebellion against her. At the same time he pleaded with the people to repent and then to hold firmly to their Protestant faith. He preached with much success throughout the fall, even though it became increasingly dangerous as Queen Mary's government became more threatening.

Returning to London, Knox married Marjory Bowes, to whom he had become engaged several years earlier. Her father, a Catholic, bitterly opposed the marriage. But Marjory's mother supported them and had great affection for Knox, who in turn always showed his respect for her, calling her his mother.

After the marriage they could not settle in Berwick, because Knox saw no way to support himself. The allowance he had received as a chaplain in King Edward's court stopped when Mary became queen. His father-in-law was wealthy, but Knox would not accept support from a man who treated him disdainfully.

At this time national affairs moved rapidly against Protestants. Parliament repealed all the laws that had been made in favor of the Reformation and restored Catholicism as the official religion of the nation. It did allow observance of Protestant worship until December 20, 1553. After that, Protestants were to be treated as heretics.

Many ministers escaped from England, but Knox would neither flee nor stop preaching. His enemies had not been able to ruin him previously, as long as he had been under King Edward's protection. Now they had the new government's support in trying to accuse him. They intercepted letters from him to his wife and mother-in-law, hoping to find support for their charges.

Knox knew his letters contained only personal greetings and urgings to his friends to remain true to their Protestant faith, statements he continually made in public for all to hear. But he was concerned for his family and friends and determined to visit them. Other friends convinced him of his danger in making such a trip. They found a safe retreat for him on the coast where he could escape by sea if necessary.

He wrote his wife from this refuge that his friends had compelled him to hide against his wishes, "for never could I die in a more honest quarrel than by suffering as a witness for that truth of which God has made me a messenger."

Finally Knox was convinced that he could never escape his enemies if he remained in England. He left the country in January 1554, going to Dieppe; from there, he could quickly return to either Scotland or England if circumstances permitted.

3

By yielding to the urgent pleas of his friends, Knox had followed the scriptural injunction, "When they persecute you in this city, flee ye into another" (Matthew 10:23). But he regretted the step he had been induced to take, preferring, as a man of courage, to face danger with his friends. But they knew he was too valuable to the Protestant cause to risk his life unnecessarily.

He wrote his mother-in-law, "England and Scotland shall both know that I am ready to suffer more than either poverty or exile for the profession of that doctrine and that heavenly religion, whereof it has pleased His merciful providence to make me, among others, a simple soldier and witness-bearer unto men."

In his forced exile, he subjected himself and his ministry to severe scrutiny, dedicating himself to a more devoted course of action in the future. Those who knew him best would have thought it impossible for him to be more devoted to the Protestant cause than he had been.

While in exile, he wrote two short treatises, which he sent to England. One was a practical exposition of Psalm 6; the other, a lengthy letter to those in London and other parts of England who had heard him preach. The letter eloquently warned them against taking part in the Catholic observances that had been reinstated, and urged them to remain true to the Protestant faith.

In February 1554, Knox traveled through France to Switzerland, welcomed there by sympathizing friends who regretted the overthrow of Protestantism in England. He visited the Swiss churches and conferred with Protestant leaders of the country, while keeping in constant touch with events in England. In Geneva he formed a friendship with John Calvin, which lasted until Calvin's death ten years later. Knox met many distinguished men from England, France, Germany, Poland, Hungary, Spain, and Italy who thronged Geneva at that time. They came to consult Calvin about the progress of the Reformation, or to find shelter from the persecutions sweeping their countries.

Knox and Calvin were nearly the same age. They had similar beliefs and strength of purpose. Knox's piety and talents impressed

Calvin; Knox, in turn, had a higher opinion of Calvin than of any other Reformer. Knox approved of the religious order Calvin had established in the government of Geneva and decided to make the city his headquarters until he could return to England.

In July 1554, he went back to Dieppe to find out what was happening in England and Scotland. The news was discouraging. Mary Stuart, the infant Queen, had been sent to France for safety, and her mother, Mary of Lorraine, was regent in Scotland. She and Mary Tudor, queen of England, were Catholics. Knox was convinced that both of those countries were closed to him for the time being. He was discouraged also to learn that some of his converts had gone back to observing the Roman Catholic mass. Out of this dark picture came his "Admonition to England," a strong denunciation of the religious policies of the government. Its stinging language condemned the cruel persecution of Protestants in England.

Returning to Geneva, Knox threw himself into his studies, and, although nearly fifty years old, he mastered the Hebrew language. His income was extremely limited, though friends in England and Scotland gave him financial help from time to time.

Great numbers of Protestants fled England by the end of 1554, finding a warm welcome in the European cities of Zurich, Basel, Frankfurt, Strassburg, and Geneva. A French

Protestant group in Frankfurt gave the English settlers permission to use its church as a place of worship.

The English members elected three pastors, giving them equal authority. They asked Knox to be one of the pastors and, at Calvin's urging, he accepted the call. Difficulties among the congregation arose within a few months over the use of the *Book of Common Prayer,* and Knox resigned. He was driven away by false accusations that he plotted treason against the emperor of Germany and Queen Mary of England. The city fathers privately supported Knox but urged him to leave the city for his own safety and for the sake of peace. He returned to Geneva, where Calvin warmly welcomed him, making it plain that he thought Knox had been treated in an unchristian way.

Then, hearing that a favorable change had taken place in the situation of Protestants in Scotland, Knox immediately sailed for England. He stopped in Berwick first to visit his wife, whom he had not seen for two years. Continuing to hear encouraging reports, he went to Edinburgh and began preaching in the house where he lived. Many, including nobles, came to listen, intensely interested in what they heard. Knox traveled constantly in different parts of the country and made converts from the nobility. As a result, the clergy became alarmed at his preaching and at the rapid spread of Reformed doctrines.

They ordered him to appear before a convention of clergy in Edinburgh, not expecting him to obey. When he agreed to do so, his enemies dared not meet him and canceled the convention. Knox returned to Edinburgh and preached to greater crowds than before.

In the midst of these preaching opportunities in Scotland, the English church in Geneva invited him to come as one of its pastors. Some of the members of the Geneva church had been in the Frankfurt church, but had come to Geneva for greater freedom of worship. Knox was encouraged by this public testimony to his integrity from some who had been in the Frankfurt church and who knew why he had left it. He accepted the invitation, even though friends in Scotland begged him to remain there. He promised he would return if he were needed, and in July 1556 went to Geneva with his wife and her mother.

As soon as he was gone, his ecclesiastical enemies again ordered him to appear before them, knowing he was not there to do so. They "condemned his body to the flames and his soul to damnation." Since both were beyond their reach, they had to be satisfied with burning him in effigy.

The burning prompted him to write "The Appellation," addressed to both the nobles and common people of Scotland. It was a vigorous treatise, setting forth the doctrines

Knox had taught while in Scotland, against which the clergy were so vehement.

Knox taught that there is no other name by which men can be saved but that of Jesus, and that all reliance on the merits of others is vain. Since the Savior has by His one sacrifice sanctified and reconciled to God those who should inherit the promised kingdom, all other sacrifices that men pretend to offer for sin are blasphemous. All men ought to hate sin, which is so odious to God that no sacrifice but the death of His Son could satisfy for it. Men ought to magnify their heavenly Father, who did not spare Him who is the substance of His glory, but gave Him up to suffer the ignominious and cruel death of the cross for us. Those who have been washed from their former sins are bound to lead a new life, fighting against the lusts of the flesh and trying to glorify God by good works.

He further taught that it is obligatory for those who hope for life everlasting to make an open profession of the doctrine of Christ, and to avoid idolatry, superstition, vain religion, and every way of worship that is destitute of authority from the Word of God. This doctrine agreed so clearly with the Word of God that he thought no one could deny any part of it. Yet the false bishops and ungodly clergy had condemned him as a heretic and his doctrine as heretical. They had pronounced against him the sentence of death and burned his effigy. He appealed this sentence to a lawful council to be held in conformity with ancient laws and canons. He humbly requested that the nobility and commons of Scotland take him, and others who were accused and persecuted, under their protection until these controversies were decided.

Knox's visit to Scotland had laid the foundation for a work that could not be completed then because the time was not ripe. Therefore, his move back to Geneva was a wise step. It not only preserved his life for a later ministry, but also deflected a storm of persecution from fellow believers.

His two-year stay in Geneva was one of the most peaceful and comfortable times of his life. Two sons were born to him and his wife. In addition to a happy home life, he enjoyed the friendship of Calvin and other Reformers.

During those years he sent two letters to Scotland. One was written to all Protestants in the land, urging them to practice purity in all they did. Knox also warned them against a new sect, the Anabaptists, who were almost as opposed to the Reformed group as were the Catholics. The Anabaptists he warned against were a fanatical German group who practiced licentious living. They were not the same as the Anabaptists of Great Britain and America.

His second letter was written to the Protestant nobles, urging them to Christianize their views and purify their minds from selfish and worldly interests. He also gave them his advice on the delicate question of resistance to rulers. He had heard the report that a rebellion was planned in Scotland, and he solemnly warned all Protestants to avoid involvement in it and to beware of helping those who tried to promote their own selfish ends by overthrowing the government.

At the same time he did not retract the principle he had outlined in previous letters, that it was lawful to resist the tyrannical measures of rulers. But subjects must not resort to open resistance until they were driven to it by extreme, oppressive acts. He thought it especially necessary for Protestants in Scotland to be circumspect in all they did in order to avoid giving their adversaries a reason to accuse them of using religious reform as an excuse for sedition. However, if they were violently treated while peaceably engaging in religious observances, they did not have to stand by and see innocent people murdered; they were justified in defending themselves and others.

Early in 1558 Knox made a new translation of the Bible into English, assisted by several educated men in his congregation. It was called the Geneva Bible, after the place where it was composed and printed. It was then also that Knox published his letter to the queen regent of Scotland. Along with his former treatises, the *Appellation* and the *Exhortation,* the letter contributed to the spread of Reformed doctrines.

The most extraordinary of Knox's treatises, *The First Blast of the Trumpet Against the Monstrous Regiment of Women,* caused a great outcry. The work fiercely attacked the practice of allowing women to govern nations. Knox had held this view for some time, but had not spoken out until he was provoked by the increasing cruelties of Mary the queen of England. In the *Blast* he gave many reasons why women should not be entrusted with public authority. He supported his opinion by appealing to the constitutions of ancient free states as well as the example of France, which excluded women from the throne.

Knox was fully aware that his treatise would be unpopular and expose him to the resentment of the queens under whom he lived, Mary queen of Scots and Mary queen of England. The treatise provoked anger when Elizabeth came to the throne later in England. John Fox, the author of the *Book of Martyrs,* strongly remonstrated with Knox on the severity of the language and the impropriety of its publication. Knox had intended to write three "blasts," but because he wanted to strengthen Elizabeth's hand instead of diminish it, he relinquished the idea. However, nothing induced him to change his beliefs.

The following year an answer to the *Blast* appeared anonymously. The author, John Aylmer, an English refugee living on the continent, agreed with Knox as far as Queen Mary was concerned, but protested Elizabeth's being included. The result of the controversy was that Knox found it difficult to get permission to visit England.

Knox's letter to the Scottish nobles had the desired effect of strengthening them in their allegiance to the Protestant faith. They renewed their invitation to Knox to return to Scotland. The nobles had met in Edinburgh in December 1557 and unanimously resolved to support the Reformed doctrine and urge its acceptance by others.

Meanwhile desperate efforts were underway to crush the Reformation in Scotland. In the attempt, Walter Mill, an eighty-two-year-old former parish priest, was burned at the stake as a heretic. This barbarous and illegal execution aroused the horror and anger of the nation against the clergy to an incredible pitch, leading many to come out boldly for the new doctrines and to assemble more openly for Protestant worship.

Then, with the death of Mary queen of England and the accession of Elizabeth, Protestant refugees returned from Europe. Knox sent letters by some of them to Elizabeth's court, asking permission to travel through England on his way to Scotland. He left his wife and family in Geneva until he could be sure of their safety in Scotland. Arriving in Dieppe, he was deeply hurt at the word that the English government refused his travel request because of false charges that he and his friends were hostile to Elizabeth. He was tempted to issue his even stronger second *Blast* but decided against it because of the urgency of the situation in Scotland.

Knox had always distrusted the seeming tolerance of the queen regent of Scotland toward her Protestant subjects. His distrust was confirmed by reports that the immediate suppression of the Reformation in Scotland and its soon suppression in England were planned.

The queen regent's brothers schemed to claim the throne of England for the young queen of Scots, attack Elizabeth on the grounds that she was illegitimate and a heretic, suppress the Reformation, and establish French influence in Scotland in preparation for an attack on England's dominions. In his travels through France, Knox had become acquainted with people in the court and so learned of the plan. He was convinced that the Scottish Reformers could not resist French power alone, and that English help was needed. But he was afraid England would not help unless the queen realized the full extent of the plot and saw that it was to England's best interest to help the Scottish Protestants.

Deeply disturbed by this scheming against the Protestant religion, Knox wrote a letter to Secretary Cecil requesting permission to come to England. He insisted that he did not want to stay but had urgent matters to communicate, matters so serious they could not be put in writing.

It is to Knox's credit that he persisted in his efforts to alert England to its potential peril. The assistance Elizabeth eventually gave the Scottish Protestants was dictated by a sound policy. It defeated the plans of the enemy; gave her an influence in Scotland that her predecessors had not been able to secure by war or bribery; and stabilized her government by strengthening and supporting Protestant interests.

Knox, uncertain of Elizabeth's response, sailed from Dieppe in 1559. He landed safely in Scotland and did not leave his native land again for any prolonged period.

4

The times were critical in Scotland when Knox arrived, but he was made for critical times. He threw himself into the work of the Reformation and immediately became the life and soul of the movement. The queen regent had discarded her mask of tolerance; as a result, the Lords of the Congregation, as the Protestant nobility called itself, openly revolted against her.

As long as the queen had needed their assistance in furthering the designs of her son-in-law, the dauphin of France, she had listened to their plans for reform and apparently sympathized with them. But, having achieved her aims, her duplicity became clear. The lords were furious at this duplicity. They had agreed to her request to restrain their preachers from teaching in public and had held back a petition they had intended to present to Parliament. Now, by alienating these noblemen, her double-dealing ultimately strengthened the new faith.

The useless negotiations between the Lords of the Congregation and the Regent's Council broke off, resulting in increasing religious problems. Archbishop Hamilton received assurances from the regent that she would support his efforts to maintain the authority of the Roman church. As a result, a proclamation in Edinburgh prohibited any person from preaching or administering the sacraments without authority from the bishops. It commanded all subjects of the realm to observe Easter according to the rites of the Catholic church. When some preachers disobeyed this order, they were summoned to stand trial at Stirling. They were charged with usurping the ministerial office, administering Communion in a manner different from the Catholic church, bringing people together to preach false doctrines, and inciting them to riot.

Some of the Protestant nobles remonstrated with the regent. She replied haughtily that "in spite of them, all their preachers should be banished" from Scotland. When the nobles reminded her of her promises of protection, she answered, "Subjects have not the right to burden their princes with promises further than they please to keep them."

The nobles insisted that if she violated her agreements with her subjects, they would consider themselves absolved from any allegiance to her. When the nobles continued to vigorously remonstrate, she assumed a milder tone and agreed to suspend the trial of the preachers. Then, learning that France and Spain had mutually agreed to extirpate heretics, and hearing of Protestant worship in the city of Perth, the queen became enraged. She abruptly ordered the accused preachers to appear in Stirling for their trial.

Just at this time Knox arrived in Scotland, and the clergy were panic-stricken at his presence in the country. The queen regent immediately proclaimed him an outlaw and a rebel. Ignoring the sentence, Knox decided to accompany the accused ministers to their trial. A large group of Protestants traveled with him as far as Perth, stopping there to send word to the queen that they came peacefully. When the queen promised to stop the trial, the Protestants did not go on to Stirling. Once again the queen broke her word and when the day of the trial arrived, she ordered the prosecution to proceed. The preachers were outlawed for not appearing; everyone was forbidden to assist them in any way under pain of rebellion; those nobles who had befriended the accused were fined.

An unfortunate uprising resulted at Perth. The day the news came of the queen's change of mind, Knox preached a sermon exposing the idolatry of the mass and of image worship. After the service the audience quietly dispersed, leaving only a few people loitering in the church. A priest entered and, perhaps to show his contempt of the doctrine just preached, uncovered a rich altar piece, decorated with images, and prepared to celebrate mass. A boy objected and was struck by the priest. The boy retaliated by throwing a stone, which broke one of the images. This inflamed the people standing near, and they joined in destroying the altar and trampling on the images. The noise brought a mob and neither preachers nor authorities could restrain its fury until all the monasteries in the town lay in ruins. None of the nobles or the sensible members of the congregation took part. Only the lowest of the town's inhabitants or, as Knox put it, "the rascal multitude," did the damage.

But Knox was blamed for the destruction of the monasteries, his enemies claiming that such senseless carnage was the direct result of his preaching. The queen regent seized the opportunity to turn public anger from herself and to direct it against the Protestants. She inflamed the minds of both Catholic and Protestant moderates and, by magnifying the Perth tumult into a dangerous, planned rebellion, she collected an army and marched against Perth. The inhabitants insisted they had no plans of rebellion and tried to turn away her wrath. Finding this impossible, they decided not to let themselves be massacred at the queen's command. They rallied and defended themselves so vigorously that the queen had to sue for peace. But, allowed to enter Perth, she showed her double-dealing again by ruthlessly trampling on the conditions for peace. The young earl of Argyle and the prior of Saint Andrews deserted her, never again trusting her promises.

The leading Protestants also did not trust the queen and circulated copies of their religious covenant for signatures to determine how many friends they had. Some of the undecided nobles now associated themselves with the Reformers, whereas others remained neutral.

The Lords of the Congregation determined to deal with the scandalous lives of the Roman clergy, their total neglect of the religious instruction of the people, and other flagrant abuses. The lords abolished the Catholic order of service and set up the Reformed order of worship in every place where they had influence. They did this in response to the loudly expressed desire for these reforms by the majority of the nation.

They decided to begin the reform measures at Saint Andrews. However, the archbishop recruited armed forces and told Knox that the soldiers would fire on him and his associates if he attempted to preach in the cathedral. The noblemen with Knox had only a handful of supporters and, fearing for his life, advised him to submit to the demand. But it was at such a time, when weakness might have ruined his cause, that Knox's courage was evident. Remembering the efforts of the past years, which seemed now to be at the moment of fulfillment, he resisted his friends' pleas. He had never before preached with the thought of intentionally hurting anyone, but his conscience would not allow him to keep still on this occasion. He insisted on preaching the next day, no matter what the result.

In this town and church God first raised me to the dignity of a preacher. From it I was driven out by French tyranny at the instigation of Scottish bishops. Through all the months of imprisonment and torture I have had the confident hope of preaching once again at Saint Andrews. Now, when Providence has brought me, beyond all men's expectations, to this place, let no man hinder me. As for the fear of danger that may come to me, let no man be solicitous. My life is in the custody of Him whose glory I seek. I desire the hand or weapon of no man to defend me. I only crave opportunity to speak. If it be denied me here, I must seek it where I may find it.

This courageous stand silenced all objections, and Knox preached the next day, June 14, 1559, to a large crowd, including clergy, without the slightest interruption. He used the opportunity to expose the enormous corruptions Catholicism had brought into the church and to point out what Christians could do to remove them. As a result of his sermons over the next three days, Reformed worship was established in the town without any problems. The people stripped the church of images and demolished the monasteries. Within a few weeks other towns followed the example set in Saint Andrews and abolished Catholic worship.

The forces of the Lords of the Congregation expelled the royal garrison from Perth and seized Stirling. By the end of June they arrived in Edinburgh, forcing the queen regent to flee. Knox was with them and immediately preached in Saint Giles's and in the Abbey Church. In July the citizens of Edinburgh chose him as their minister. He accepted the election and began his work at once.

However, the queen regent's forces recovered and advanced on Edinburgh so quickly that the Protestants had to submit to a treaty and agree to leave the city. Knox wanted to remain with his congregation, but the Lords of the Congregation insisted on his leaving with them for his own safety. The queen tried to reestablish the Roman Catholic services in the church of Saint Giles, but the people refused to allow it. During the time her forces controlled Edinburgh, mass was celebrated only in the Royal Chapel and in the Church of Holyrood.

Knox made a preaching tour through Scotland, greatly encouraging and strengthening the people in their Protestant principles. In September his wife and family arrived from Geneva. The efforts of the English ambassador in France gained permission for Mrs. Knox and the family to travel through England. The English government began to regard Knox somewhat more favorably as they understood his important position with the Reformers.

Knox knew that the queen regent, aided by French money and soldiers, would overwhelm the Reformers unless they could get English aid. The queen had between three thousand and four thousand trained soldiers. Though only five hundred were Scots, her forces were constantly augmented by troops from France. The Lords of the Congregation had about eight thousand men, but only one thousand were trained soldiers.

Knox wrote Secretary Cecil, begging aid. Cecil, who was friendly to the Reformed view, exerted his influence on Elizabeth and her council. Knox received a message, asking him to meet an English messenger on secret and important business. He went to Berwick, rather than into Eng'nd, and there received the dispatches from the English government. Unfortunately the reply showed reluctance to aid the Scots, disappointing the Lords of the Congregation. Knox finally persuaded them to let him write again in his own name. His second attempt was successful, and England promised to supply both men and money. At the time so few lay Reformers were capable of conducting political negotiations, that for a long time the whole weight of the distasteful burden fell on Knox. He persevered in spite of the strong prejudice against him by Elizabeth and the English court.

Secretary Cecil insisted that Knox be involved in the financial transactions to be sure that the money was applied to "the common action" and not put to anyone's private use.

Knox became so conspicuous for his zeal and activity that the Roman Catholics offered a reward to anyone who would kill him. Though Knox knew some would try for the reward, he did not change his fearless discharge of his duties, but worked night and day for the cause to which he was committed. His bravery and wise counsel, both in public and private, greatly encouraged the other Reformers and kept them unified. Knox was himself encouraged by strong converts to the cause. The most important of these was the former regent, the duke of Chatelherault, who followed the example of his oldest son and threw in his lot with the Lords of the Congregation.

A serious question now arose concerning how to depose the queen regent. Knox's advice was sought. He reminded the lords that when they had first taken arms, it was not to change the government or take it over, but simply to defend themselves. Even though they resisted the queen regent, they continued to recognize her position as regent, presented petitions to her, and listened respectfully to the proposals she made to settle the differences between them. But, discovering that she planned to take away their national liberties, which as queen she could do, they were forced to change their tactics.

Knox further reminded them that their true rulers were minors living in a foreign country and under the control of the very people who were responsible for the problems the lords faced. Since the queen regent held her position by the authority of Parliament, she could be deprived of it by the same authority. Since the state of the country made it impossible for a free Parliament to meet, and the majority of the people were dissatisfied with her rule, it was the lords' responsibility to provide for the public safety.

The situation was hotly discussed. Finally, after much deliberation, a large group of nobles, barons, and representatives of the various boroughs, met in Edinburgh in October 1559 to decide the important issue. Knox and another Protestant minister were asked to give their opinion as to the lawfulness of the proposed measure. Their judgment, based on Scripture and logic, was that the power of rulers, being limited, could be taken away if there were valid grounds. The queen regent had shown her determination to suppress and enslave the kingdom by bringing foreign troops into the country, so the nobles and barons had the right to take away her authority, since she had repeatedly rejected their petitions and remonstrances.

Knox added that the assembly acted within its rights, provided it remembered three things. First, the members were not to allow the misconduct of the queen regent to change their allegiance to the rightful sovereigns, Francis and Mary. Second, the council members were not to be motivated by private envy or hatred of the queen regent, but only by thoughts of the safety of the Commonwealth. Third, any sentence they pronounced could be changed if the queen regent afterward became sorry for her conduct.

After deliberation, the whole assembly suspended the Queen from her authority as regent of the kingdom until a free Parliament could meet. It elected a council for the temporary management of public affairs. Four Protestant ministers, one of them Knox, were appointed to assist the council in determining religious affairs.

Some later objected that ministers of the gospel were incompetent to decide the question of deposing the queen regent. But the ministers could not refuse to give their opinion when asked, especially when the question involved conscience as well as law and political right.

Knox believed, as did the English patriots of the later time of Charles I, that a mutual compact, tacit and implied if not formal and explicit, existed between rulers and their subjects. If rulers flagrantly violated that compact and became habitual tyrants and notorious oppressors, then the people were absolved from their allegiance. Subjects had the right to resist such rulers, formally depose them, and elect others in their place.

To the Reformers' dismay, the situation did not improve as they had hoped it would after the queen regent was deposed. The messenger they sent to the English court was robbed of the money he brought back; their soldiers mutinied because they were not paid; and French troops routed them in a skirmish. The queen regent's secret agents were constantly at work among the discontented Protestants. With desertions occurring thick and fast, the discouraged remnant who remained true to the faith abandoned Edinburgh hastily and retreated to Stirling.

Almost alone, Knox still hoped against hope. From his pulpit at Stirling he preached a powerful sermon that rekindled the spirits of the Lords of the Congregation. They had been trusting too much, he said, in the arm of flesh, especially since influential nobles had joined their cause. So God had allowed these disasters to fall upon them momentarily in order to bring them back to Him, their eternal refuge and strength. Their cause might seem weak at the time, but it would eventually triumph.

After the sermon, the council members, their faith renewed, agreed to send a messenger to London to beg more active support from Queen Elizabeth. The council divided itself into two parts, one to be stationed at Glasgow, the other at Saint Andrews. Knox went to Saint Andrews in the double capacity of preacher and secretary. A French fleet tried to storm Saint Andrews, but Knox encouraged resistance in hopes that the English fleet would arrive and force the enemy to retreat.

The appeal to England brought results. Elizabeth and her council concluded a treaty with the Lords of the Congregation, agreeing to assist them in expelling the French forces. Hearing this, the queen regent ordered her forces to attack the Reformers at Glasgow. But her soldiers retreated when they heard that English soldiers were marching toward Scotland.

The English army and the soldiers of the Lords of the Congregation joined forces to surround Leith by land and sea and force the French to surrender. While the seige was in progress, the queen regent unexpectedly died in Edinburgh Castle, bringing a great change in political events.

Up to this time Elizabeth had been lukewarm in her support of the Scots, but she finally decided to pursue the war vigorously. This action, combined with political difficulties in France, forced the French cabinet to conclude a treaty with England. It provided that French troops be immediately withdrawn, and that amnesty be granted all who had resisted the late queen regent. It also provided that the principal grievances of the people be corrected; that a free Parliament be held to settle the affairs of the kingdom; and that a council, chosen partly by Francis and Mary and partly by the Estates of the realm, should administer the government. This treaty ended the civil war and gave victory to the Scottish Reformation.

The Protestants had made such headway in Scotland that they were the most powerful party in the nation, both in numbers and in influence. They were happy to have the settlement of the religious question in their own hands. The Estates of Parliament met in August with a great crowd gathering peacefully in Edinburgh. Many of the Catholic lords stayed away, although the archbishop of Saint Andrews and other Catholic leaders took part in the proceedings.

A Protestant petition signed by persons of all ranks asked Parliament for legislation on three specific points. First, that the antichristian doctrines of the Roman Catholic church be discarded. Second, that purity of worship and primitive discipline be restored. Finally, that church moneys that had maintained the corrupt church hierarchy now be used to support godly ministers, to promote learning, and to help the poor. The petitioners were prepared to prove that many of the clergy were not fit to be called ministers of religion, and that they could no longer be tolerated in a Reformed commonwealth.

Parliament asked the Reformed ministers to present a summary of their doctrines with proof that they were scriptural. In reply, the ministers collaborated to write a Confession of Faith, which was similar

51

to confessions already published by other Reformed groups. It professed belief in the same articles of Christianity as did the church of Rome concerning God's nature, the Trinity, the creation of the world, the origin of evil, and the person of Christ. However, the confession condemned the idolatrous, superstitious tenets of the Roman Catholic church and also its deviation from Scripture regarding man's sinful condition and the means of salvation.

The confession was read first before the Lords of Articles and then before the whole Parliament. Protestant ministers were present in the House to defend it if attacked and to answer any questions concerning it.

Those who had objections were asked to state them. The vote on the acceptance of the confession was delayed a day to give ample time for discussion. Then the confession was read, article by article. Only a few of the nobles voted negatively, reasoning thus: "We will believe as our forefathers believed."

After the vote establishing the Confession of Faith, one of the nobles declared that the silence of the clergy had convinced him of the truth of the Protestant doctrine. He declared that no one in the future could argue against the confession, since ample time had been given for discussion and no one had objected to it.

So on August 24, 1560, Parliament abolished the papal jurisdiction in Scotland, prohibited the celebration of the mass, and revoked all laws formerly made in support of the Roman Catholic church and against the Reformed faith.

Protestantism was formally established as the religion of Scotland, largely because of John Knox's courageous efforts and his willingness to suffer persecution. At that time there was no other person in Scotland whose word was everywhere regarded with such respect and reverence.

5

The Reformers had taken the first steps toward settling the religious difficulties, and now they were eager to provide religious instruction for everyone in the kingdom. They realized the importance of church discipline in furthering the spread of religion, maintaining order, and preserving sound doctrine and morals. Knox was firm on the matter of church discipline, for he had seen in England the sad results of the lack of such discipline.

Consequently, immediately after Parliament was dissolved, the Privy Council commissioned Knox and the four ministers who had worked with him on the confession to draw up a plan of ecclesiastical government. They began at once, carefully and diligently drawing their principles and ordinances from Scripture alone. The resulting document is known as *The First Book of Discipline.*

The document set out in careful detail the form and order of the Protestant Church of Scotland. It provided for four kinds of permanent officers of the church. The minister or pastor preached the gospel and administered the sacraments. The doctor or teacher interpreted Scripture and was responsible for refuting error, including those who taught theology in schools and universities. The third officer was the ruling elder who assisted the minister in carrying out church discipline and government. The deacon was the fourth officer and he had the oversight of the moneys of the church and was responsible for the care of the poor.

In addition to those officers, the times required men in unusual and temporary positions. There was not a sufficient number of ministers to spread through the country to lead the people in public worship and to instruct them. So godly men who had some education were appointed and called readers to read the Scriptures and lead in prayer. In large parishes added responsibilities were given to men who showed themselves capable of learning. They were carefully examined and then allowed to add words of exhortation to the reading of the Scriptures, and so were called exhorters.

The scarcity of ministers resulted in

another temporary expedient. Instead of all being assigned to particular charges, some of the ministers were made overseers of large districts. These men traveled regularly to preach, plant churches, and inspect the conduct of the ministers, readers, and exhorters. Ten such superintendents were proposed, but the lack of the right kind of men and the lack of funds to support them resulted in the appointment of only five. When additional help was needed, the General Assembly appointed special positions.

However, no one was allowed to preach or administer the sacraments until he was specifically called to that responsibility. A man was given the pastoral office only after being elected freely by the people, examined by the ministers, and publicly admitted to the office in the presence of the congregation. On the day the candidate appeared, the presiding minister preached a sermon appropriate to the occasion. Then he questioned the candidate regarding his faith, his willingness to undertake the responsibilities of the office, the purity of his motives, and his earnestness to faithfully discharge the duties of the position. If satisfactory answers were given, and if the congregation agreed, the man was admitted and set apart by prayer without the laying-on of hands. The service concluded with another sermon, the singing of a psalm, and the benediction.

Ministers, elders, and deacons managed the affairs of each congregation. These men formed the church session, meeting regularly each week or oftener if church business required. A weekly meeting in larger towns gathered ministers and other learned men in the vicinity to expound the Scriptures. This later became the Presbytery, meeting less often, and having oversight of church affairs in a larger area. In addition, the General Assembly met at regular intervals to attend to business of the national church.

The ministers conducted public worship according to the *Book of Common Order*, adapting it when necessary to the situation in Scotland. People attended church twice on Sundays, morning and afternoon. Those needing instruction attended catechism instead of the afternoon preaching service. In towns a sermon was given one day of the week in addition to Sunday, and people could gather almost every day to hear the Scriptures read and prayer offered. Baptism was always accompanied by preaching or catechizing. The Lord's Supper was administered four times a year in the towns, with two ministrations: the first time early in the morning and another later in the day. The Reformers abolished all observances of the Roman church, such as the use of the sign of the cross in baptizing, kneeling at the Lord's table, and holy days.

The compilers of the *First Book of Discipline* showed their concern for education. They ordered that a school be established in every parish to instruct young people in religion, grammar, and Latin. They wanted a college established in every good-sized town to teach more advanced subjects. They apparently wanted to revive the system of some ancient republics in which the youth were considered the responsibility of the public rather than the parents. This system required the wealthy to educate their own children and then help educate poorer children who showed aptitude for learning. Those reforms, though proposed, did not take place as hoped because of the greed of the wealthy, who refused to cooperate.

So the church had to supply the funds to put these important measures into effect. The compilers of the *Book of Discipline* proposed that the patrimony of the Roman church should be appropriated. They argued that the Roman hierarchy had been abolished, and its clergy had been proven unfit for their positions. Since the laws of Parliament prohibited any others from assuming those positions, no one in the country had a rightful claim to that money. Therefore the Roman church revenues were to be used by the new church governing body to support the ministry, the schools, and the poor. They left undecided the way to help the poor until they could determine in each parish who were the truly needy and who were simply idle beggars.

But they were very careful to stipulate the salary that ministers, superintendents, and teachers should receive. It was to be enough for them to live on adequately, but not enough to encourage luxury. The money for salaries was to come from the tithes the people paid. But care was urged that no one, and farmers in particular, be pressured unfairly to give; the clergy had often done this in the past. The Reformers also urged that the money from rents and revenues coming from cathedrals and monasteries and other religious foundations be divided and used to support universities and churches.

These measures were extremely unpalatable to many of the Protestant nobles and others who were wealthy. Some of them had long coveted the rich revenues— both money and property—of the Roman clergy. Some had already seized church lands and hoped that seizure would be legalized. Hence their aversion to having the *Book of Discipline* ratified. This lack of cooperation from some of the Protestant nobles caused poverty among ministers and kept the universities lacking sufficient funds.

Calvin, the Swiss Reformer, by his eloquence and firmness had succeeded in helping his countrymen to overcome their desire for gain and to give all of the revenues of the Roman church in their country to the Protestant cause. Knox did not find it as easy to manage the turbulent and powerful nobles of Scotland. The demands of the Reformers for the funds formerly given to the Roman church were not extravagant or unreasonable. They did not want the money for their own selfish interests, but for the support of the ministry and education.

The greedy Protestant nobles who saw no hope of personal financial gain, spoke sneeringly of the provisions of the *Book of Discipline* as "devote imaginations." So, when the plan was submitted to the Privy Council, they opposed it strongly, even though other members approved it. Eventually the document was approved, submitted to the nation for its acceptance, and most of the regulations concerning the church were put into effect. But the Estates of Parliament did not approve either the *First Book of Discipline* or the *Second Book of Discipline,* compiled twenty years later.

The first meeting of the General Assembly of the church of Scotland was held at Edinburgh in December 1560. It consisted of forty members, only six of whom were ministers, with Knox as the leading spirit. The assembly passed regulations concerning the constituent members of the court, the causes that ought to come before them, and the manner of procedure they ought to follow.

Before the end of the year, Knox was crushed by his wife's death. She had shared the hardships of exile with him, but died soon after reaching her native land, leaving him with two young children. Knox's mother-in-law's grief heightened his anxieties, for she fell into deep despondency. Calvin wrote him a touching letter of sympathy.

In addition to domestic troubles, public problems flared. Although the Reformation had made rapid progress, Mary queen of Scots and her husband, the king of France, refused to ratify the treaty that had ended the civil war. They dismissed the deputy who represented the Reformers in Parliament, highly displeased at the religious innovations that were introduced into Scotland. News came that a new army was preparing in France to invade Scotland in the spring and that emissaries were coming in advance of the invasion to encourage and unite Catholics. Knox contemplated the future with foreboding; it was not clear whether Elizabeth would intervene a second time to help the Scots. Fortunately, the threat of invasion blew over when the French king died.

However, another danger came to the

Scottish Reformed church almost at once. The Protestant nobles invited the young queen to come to Scotland after her husband's death and take the reins of government into her own hands. She did so, arriving in August 1561.

Knox described the day of her arrival. "The very face of the heavens, the time of her arrival, did manifestly speak what was brought into this country with her, to wit, sorrow, darkness, dolor, and all impiety. In the memory of man, that day of the year was never seen a more dolorous face of heaven, which two days after did so continue. . . . The sun was not seen to shine two days after. That forewarning God gave unto us, but alas the most part were blind."

Though the majority of the people responded to her coming with joy, Knox mourned that, "Fires of joy were set forth at night and a company of most honest men, with instruments of music and with musicians, gave their salutations at her chamber windows." He regretted that Protestant nobles, along with others, came to show their respects.

However, consternation came to many the following Sunday when the queen celebrated the mass in her apartments. When it became known, many protested, but some of the Protestant nobles intervened to protect the priests. Knox and others made it clear that they would not tolerate the idolatry to pollute the land that God had used them to exterminate.

It was soon apparent that an immense gulf separated Mary and the Reformers. All the old dissensions revived along with new ones. The queen was completely antagonistic to men like Knox on all questions of religion, of the relation of princes and subjects, and of the guiding principles of life. The fierce controversies between the queen and Knox showed that there was not a single point on which friendly discussion was possible.

Mary's restoring the mass horrified the Protestants. "Shall that idol be suffered to take place within this realm again? It shall not!" they exclaimed.

The loud discontent threatened open rebellion until some of the leading Reformers intervened to quiet the crowd's passion. Knox was reluctant to offend the queen so soon after her coming and hoped to preserve public peace. So he met in private with those who wanted to prevent the mass by armed force. However, he was as concerned about the situation as they were and preached a sermon saying that that "one mass was more fearful to me than if ten thousand armed enemies were landed in any part of the realm to suppress religion."

Some have called Knox and his friends

intolerant for their strong opposition to Roman Catholic practices. But they knew that public toleration of the mass would be only a first step to reestablishing the hated religion in Scotland, which would kindle afresh the fires of persecution. The Roman Catholic princes of Europe were already in league to exterminate Protestants everywhere, and the Scottish queen was in sympathy with the plans. The lords of the Privy Council had once exclaimed to the English Mary, "God forbid that the lives of the faithful should stand in the power of the papists; for past experience has taught us what cruelty is in their hearts."

Knox distrusted the Scottish Queen Mary, who had been brought up in France where she had been accustomed to seeing Protestants burned. Scotland, a Protestant nation, dared not complacently observe the Catholic doings of their queen.

A French author, discussing this point, frankly and candidly remarked, "I maintain that, in the state of men's spirits at that time, if a Huguenot queen had come to take possession of a Roman Catholic kingdom with the slender retinue with which Mary went to Scotland, the first thing they would have done would have been to arrest her; and, if she had persevered in her religion, they would have procured her degradation by the pope, thrown her into the Inquisition, and burnt her as a heretic.

There is not an honest man who can deny this."

As minister of the only Reformed church in Edinburgh, Knox considered Mary to be under his special charge. So he subjected both her personal conduct and her public policies to stringent criticism. During her entire reign, not falling under the spell of her personal beauty, his attitude was boldly and uncompromisingly antagonistic to her. He preached a sermon in Saint Giles's church against her observance of the mass in Holyrood Chapel. As a result, Mary summoned him to a personal interview.

The queen accused him of turning part of her subjects first against her mother and now against herself. She charged that his *The First Blast Against Women* had been written to oppose her just authority, and that he was the cause of much sedition and slaughter in England.

"You have done all this through magic," she concluded hotly.

Knox shattered all her arguments. He spoke boldly against the Roman Catholic mass, proving that religion took its origin and authority only from the eternal God, not from human rulers. He insisted that he had always spoken against magic and necromancy and those who practiced them.

As to the *Blast Against Women,* he said, "I have communicated my judgment to the world. If the realm finds no inconveniency in the reign of a woman, that which they approve shall I not further disallow, except within my own breast. I shall be as well content to live under your Grace, as Paul was to live under Nero. And my hope is, that so long as you defile not your hands with the blood of the saints of God, neither I nor that book shall either hurt you or your authority. That book was written most especially against that wicked Jezebel [Mary] of England."

"Do you think that subjects who have power may resist their princes?" she demanded.

"If the princes exceed their bounds and do against those things in which they should be obeyed, then they may be resisted, even by force. No greater honor or obedience should be given to kings and princes than God has commanded to be given to father and mother. If the father be stricken with a frenzy in which he would slay his own children, the children may join together, apprehend the father, take his weapons from him, bind him, and keep him in prison till his frenzy be past. Do you think, Madam, that the children do wrong? Or do you think that God will be offended with them for having kept their father from doing wickedness? It is even so with princes who would murder the children of God who are their subjects. Their blind zeal is nothing but a mad frenzy. To take the sword from them and bind their hands and cast them into prison until they be brought to a more sober mind, is not disobedience agains the rulers, but obedience because it is the will of God."

The queen was so angry that she could not immediately answer. Finally she said, "Well then, I perceive that my subjects should obey you rather than me and do what they wish, and not what I command. That means I would be subject to them and not they to me."

"God forbid, Madam, that I should ever command anyone to obey me or to tell subjects that they may do whatever pleases them. My burden is that both subjects and princes obey God. And do not think, Madam, that wrong is done you when you are counseled to be subject to God's will, for it is He who subjects people under princes and requires that they obey. God wants kings to be foster fathers to His church and queens to be nurses to His people. This subjection to God and to His troubled church is the greatest dignity that can come to man on earth, for it carries him to everlasting glory."

"But you are not the church that I will nurse," the queen answered. "I will defend the church of Rome, for it is the true church of God."

Knox thundered, "Madam, your will or

reason cannot make that Roman harlot to be the true and immaculate bride of Jesus Christ. Do not be surprised that I call Rome a harlot. That church is polluted with all kinds of spiritual fornication in doctrine and customs. I believe, Madam, that the synagogue of the Jews which crucified the Son of God was not as far degenerated from the statutes that God gave by Moses and Aaron to His people, as the church of Rome has degenerated in five hundred years from the purity of the religion which the apostles taught and planted."

"My conscience does not admit that."

"Conscience requires knowledge," he shot back. "And you have no knowledge—"

"I have both heard and read," she answered.

"The Jews who crucified Christ Jesus read both the law and the prophets and had it interpreted the way they wished. Have you heard anyone teach anything but what the pope and the cardinals allow? No one will speak anything that will jeopardize their lives or property."

"You interpret the Scripture in one way, they in another. Whom shall I believe? Who shall be the judge?"

"Madam, you shall believe God who speaks plainly in His Word. Further than the Word teaches you shall not believe the one or the other. The Word of God is plain in itself. If there is any obscurity anywhere, the Holy Spirit explains it more clearly in other places. No one can remain in doubt, save those who remain obstinately ignorant. For example, the Roman Catholics boldly affirm that the mass is the ordinance of God, instituted by Jesus Christ, and is a sacrifice for the living and the dead. We deny that and affirm that the mass, as it is now used, is the invention of man, not a sacrifice that God commanded, and therefore is an abomination to God. Who is to judge as to which of us is right? No one should be believed who can not prove his beliefs from a true witness. We must go by the plain words of Scripture. Now if they can prove by Scripture they are right, we shall grant it. But the Word of God plainly assures us that Christ Jesus did not command the mass to be said at His Last Supper, since the mass is not mentioned within the whole of Scripture."

"You are too much for me," the queen answered. "But if those were here who taught me, they could answer you."

"I would to God the most learned papist in Europe were present, Madam, as well as those whom you believe, and you would hear the arguments. I am sure that you would hear the emptiness of the Roman Catholic religion and see how little ground it has in the Word of God. But no learned papist will ever come into your presence, Madam, to have the foundation of his religion searched out. They know that they can never sustain an argument except by fire and sword and their own laws as judges. Often the papists in this and other realms have been called into conference, but they would not come unless they were judges. Therefore, Madam, I must say again that they never dare dispute unless they are both judge and party."

As the queen stood up to leave, Knox pleaded, "I pray God, Madam, that you may be blessed within the commonwealth of Scotland, if it be God's will, as Deborah was in the commonwealth of Israel."

Hearing about the interview, the godly in the land rejoiced that Mary had heard the gospel from Knox and hoped she would give heed to it. Their hopes were dashed when the queen continued to observe the mass and mocked Knox's words.

In reply to questions from his friends about the queen, Knox said, "If there be not in her a proud mind, a crafty wit, and a hard heart against God and His truth, my judgment fails me."

Knox wrote Secretary Cecil about the interview, saying that he had not seen such craft in any person of Mary's age. "She will never embrace Protestantism, for the Roman Catholic doctrines are so deeply engraven in her heart."

He determined to watch her vigilantly. The more the zeal of the Protestant nobles cooled, lulled by the queen's charm, the more persistently he warned them against her. His admonitions irritated the queen, but made her act more moderately than she otherwise would have, and they also aroused the Protestants to zeal and watchfulness.

The English ambassador, going regularly to hear Knox preach, wrote Cecil, "I assure you the voice of one man is able, in an hour, to put more life in us than six hundred trumpets blustering in our ears."

When Secretary Cecil urged Knox to be more conciliatory, he replied, "Men delighting to swim between two waters have often complained of my severity. I fear that that which men term leniency and gentleness will bring more fearful destruction than has yet fallen from the vehemence of any preacher in this realm."

Mary strongly opposed the General Assembly and wanted it suppressed. She and her nobles also bitterly denounced the *Book of Discipline.* Secretary Maitland asked scoffingly who would be subject to it. One of the Protestants insisted that all who agreed with its principles should obey it. "For to what end," he asked, "shall men subscribe, and never mean to keep word of that which they promise?"

The division of church property was another cause of dissension. Under the arrangement that had been adopted, those in actual possession of the property received two-thirds and the Reformed ministers one-third. Knox protested the settlement, not in his own interests, for he had been liberally provided for by the city authorities, but in the interest of the poor Protestant clergy.

He exclaimed, "I see two parts given to the devil, and the third must be divided betwixt God and the devil. O happy servants of the devil, and miserable servants of Jesus Christ, if after this life there were not hell and heaven."

Knox's reputation for justice and upright dealing caused him to be asked frequently to be umpire and mediator in civil disputes among Protestants. He also frequently interceded with Edinburgh's town council on behalf of those arrested for disorderly conduct. A number of nobles sought his counsel to settle feuds and family quarrels.

Knox and the queen had another stormy interview in May 1562. The French Protestants were again being persecuted. Soldiers attacked a congregation at worship, killing and mutilating men, women, and children. When the queen heard the news, she immediately gave a ball for her foreign (French) servants, the dancing lasting well into the night.

Such an outrage brought Knox's wrath. The following Sunday he preached on the text, "And now understand, O ye kings,

and be instructed, ye judges of the earth."
He attacked the ignorance, the vanity, and
the contemptuous attitude of rulers toward
those who hated vice and loved virtue.

The queen ordered the Reformer to
appear before her. When he came, he was
accused of speaking irreverently of the
queen, of having brought her into contempt, and of exceeding the bounds of his
text. Mary delivered a long harangue on
the three charges and then waited for his
reply.

"Madam, God often compels the stub-
born of the world who will not hear God
speaking to comfort the penitent and to
amend the wicked, to hear the false reports
of others to their greater displeasure. Some
reported to proud Herod that Christ Jesus
called him a fox. But they did not report
how odious it was before God that he had
murdered an innocent, which he did when
he caused John the Baptist to be beheaded
to reward the dancing of an harlot's
daughter. Madam, if the reporters of my
words had been honest men, they would
have reported my words and the circumstances of the same. But because they desire
credit at court, they must have something
to pleasure your Majesty, if it were but
flattery and lies. If you take pleasure in
any such persons, your Grace, it will turn
to your everlasting displeasure. If your
own ears had heard the whole matter of

which I spoke, if there be in you any spark of the Spirit of God or of honesty and wisdom, you could not justly have been offended at anything I said.

"Since you have heard their report, let your Grace hear me rehearse my text. 'And now, O kings, understand, and be learned, ye judges of the earth.' After I had spoken of the dignity of kings and rulers, the honor in which God placed them, and the obedience that is due them as God's lieutenants, I asked this question: What account shall princes make before the supreme Judge when they so shamefully abuse His throne and authority? The complaint of Solomon is this day true that violence and oppression occupy the throne of God here in this earth. Since murderers and oppressors boldly present themselves before kings while poor saints of God are banished, we can only say that the devil has taken possession of the throne of God which ought to be fearful to all wicked doers and a refuge to those who are innocently oppressed.

"Princes will not understand; they will not be learned as God commands them. They despise God's law; they will not understand His statutes and holy ordinances. They are more interested in fiddling and flinging than in reading or hearing God's most blessed Word. Fiddlers and flatterers—which commonly corrupt the youth—are more precious in their eyes than men of wisdom and gravity who by wholesome admonition could correct the vanity and pride unto which all men are born, but which in princes take deep root because of wicked education.

"Of dancing, Madam, I said that, although in Scripture I find no praise of it, and that profane writers term it the frenzy of those who are mad rather than sober, yet I did not utterly condemn it, provided two vices are avoided. First, that the principal vocation of life not be neglected for the pleasure of dancing. Second, that they do not dance, as the Philistines their fathers, for the pleasure they take in the displeasure of God's people. If they do so, they shall receive the reward of dancers—and that will be to drink in hell unless they speedily repent—so shall God turn their mirth into sudden sorrow. God will not always afflict His people, nor will He always wink at the tyranny of tyrants. If any man, Madam, will say that I spoke more, let him now accuse me. I think I have not only touched the sense, but the very words as I spake them."

The queen answered, "Your words are sharp enough as you have said them, but they were told to me in another way. I know that you and my uncle disagree because you are not of the same religion, and therefore I cannot blame you. But if you hear anything about me that you do not like, come and tell me and I will hear you."

"Madam, your uncles are enemies to God and to His Son Jesus Christ. They spill the blood of innocent people in order to maintain their own pomp and worldly glory. They do not spare the blood of innocents. They shall have no better success than others have before them. But as to you, Madam, I am glad to do all I can to help you, providing I do not go beyond the bounds of my vocation. I am called, Madam, to a public ministry within the church of God and am appointed by God to rebuke the sins of everyone. I am not appointed to go to every individual, for that would be an infinite labor. If your Grace pleases to come to public worship, you shall fully understand my views as to your Majesty and to all others. Or, if your Grace would like me to come at a certain time to hear the doctrine which I teach, I will gladly wait your Grace's pleasure, time, and place. But to wait at your chamber door and only have opportunity to whisper my mind in your Grace's ear, or to tell you what others think and speak of you, my conscience and the vocation God has called me to will not permit it. Just now I am here at your Grace's command, yet I do not know what others think of my neglecting my work at this time of day to wait upon the court."

The queen abruptly turned her back on him, and Knox left the court, not troubled by the conversation. Some of the Catholics were offended when they saw that he did not fear the queen. He answered, "Why should the pleasing face of a gentlewoman fear me? I have looked in the faces of angry men, and yet have not been afraid above measure."

Knox's labors were so arduous and took such a toll of his strength that an assistant pastor was provided him in 1563. Since 1560 he had preached twice each Sunday and three times during the week in Saint Giles's church, often to three thousand people. He performed all the duties of the ministerial office, met each week with the church session for discipline, and attended other meetings. The town council, with the approval of the General Assembly, appointed John Craig, a distinguished Reformer, as his assistant.

Mary still employed some Protestants as counselors. One was the prior of Saint Andrews, the earl of Murray, who was the chief director of public affairs. When Murray was married, Knox performed the ceremony before the congregation. He urged Murray to be true to the Protestant faith and not be corrupted by the court.

The Protestant counselors, however, did not have the confidence of the queen. The Roman Catholics tried every means they could to cause trouble between the queen and the Protestant nobles in an effort to ruin and displace them. Knox traveled widely to strengthen the faith of the Protestants. The earl of Murray crushed a Catholic revolt in the north of Scotland in the fall of 1562, dashing Mary's hopes of having the mass and the Catholic religion restored throughout the kingdom by the end of the year.

In September 1562, Knox debated the abbot of Crossraguel who attempted to prove that the mass originated from Melchizedek's offering bread and wine to God. In three days of discussion Knox clearly showed that the claim had no proof. About the same time a priest sent Knox a series of questions on the principal differences between Roman Catholics and Protestants. The Reformer answered many of the questions from the pulpit, especially those relating to the call of Protestant ministers.

Early in 1563 a Protestant preacher was accused of adultery. The affair caused much scandal. Knox and several elders tried the case and found the man guilty. He fled and was excommunicated, though he later repented and confessed his wrong. Appearing at the church door in sackcloth, bareheaded and barefooted, on three successive occasions, with public expressions of sorrow before the whole congregation on the final day, was the mode of public repentance afterwards used in all cases of aggravated immorality.

Knox exercised strict vigilance over the morals of Reformed ministers. He knew that much of the unpopularity of the Roman clergy came from their scandalous lives. He was doubly anxious that the people's new spiritual guides be men of pure lives and conversation.

6

While Mary was at Lochleven in May 1563, the Protestant nobles in the West made a determined stand against the Roman priests who, with Mary's protection, were again openly celebrating the mass. In accordance with the law, some of the offenders were arrested. Although this angered Mary, it did not stop the Reformers from enforcing the law.

Mary sent for Knox and spoke earnestly with him for two hours, asking him to persuade the Reformers to stop interfering with Catholic worship. He replied that if she would exercise her authority in enforcing the laws of the land, he could promise the peaceful behavior of Protestants. But if she refused, he feared the Roman priests could not flout the law, which forbade the celebration of the mass, and avoid punishment.

"Will you allow them to take *my* sword in their hands?" the queen demanded.

"The sword of justice is *God's,*" Knox replied firmly. "It is given to princes and rulers for one end which, if they transgress, sparing the wicked and oppressing the innocent, then those who in the fear of God execute judgment where God has commanded, offend not God."

Knox then reminded the queen of a doctrine that kings did not like. "Consider what it is your Grace's subjects look to receive of your Majesty, and what it is that you ought to do unto them. They are bound to obey you in obedience to God; you are bound to keep laws to them. You crave of them service; they crave of you protection and defense against wicked doers. Now, Madam, if you shall deny your duty unto them, which especially requires that you shall punish malefactors, do you think you will receive full obedience from them? I fear, Madam, you shall not."

The queen was greatly displeased, perhaps because she had no answer to his arguments. Knox was preparing early the next day to return to Edinburgh when he received a message that the queen wished to see him again. This time her attitude was completely different. She spoke softly and graciously to him, and, as a result, Knox agreed to interfere to prevent some pending church appointments. There is no question that he was deceived by Mary's empty promises. He soon found that her promise to faithfully administer the laws without fear or favor were pretense. She gave evidence of this by freeing a number of Roman Catholic priests who had been arrested for breaking the law.

Parliament met in May 1563, the first time since the queen's arrival in Scotland. Many hoped that it would act at once to ratify the treaty of peace made in July 1560 and thus legally confirm the Protestant faith. But Mary had laid her plans well. She spoke so effectively, and the self-interest of some of the Protestant nobles was so strong that the treaty was not ratified. Thus the country lost the only favorable opportunity during Mary's reign to give legal security to the Reformed faith, which would have removed one great source of national turmoil. Parliament did pass an act of oblivion, giving indemnity to those who had taken part in the civil war. But the way it was enacted implied that the treaty itself was invalid. The other acts of that Parliament were antagonistic to the Reformers.

Realizing the full extent of Mary's dissimulation, Knox was angry and demanded that the Reformers take action. They replied they could do nothing until the queen's planned marriage provided an opportunity. The selfishness and servility of these Protestant leaders grieved Knox, and the political differences severed the friendship between Knox and the earl of Murray. Knox felt that Murray had allowed his promotion in the realm to turn him from zeal for the truth.

Knox wrote Murray, "I leave you this day victor of your enemies, promoted to great honor, and in credit and authority with your sovereign. If so you long continue, none within the realm shall be more glad than I. But if after this you shall decay—as I fear you shall—then call to mind by what means God exalted you, which was neither by bearing with impiety, neither yet by maintaining of pestilent papists."

One must admire Knox's firm adherence to conscience in breaking with Murray, for the step involved great personal sacrifice. However, the queen and others rejoiced at the breach.

Before Parliament was dissolved, Knox revealed his heart before the lords in a powerful sermon in which he inveighed against the deep ingratitude that people of all ranks showed toward God's delivering them from bondage of soul and body. He made a passionate appeal to his listeners, insisting he saw nothing but a cowardly desertion of Christ's standard. Some, he said, even had the effrontery to say that they had neither law nor Parliament for their religion.

He argued back that they had the authority of God for their faith, and that God's truth was independent of human laws. He insisted that the Reformed faith was accepted within the realm by a public Parliament that had been as lawful and free as had any previous Parliament. Concluding his message, he referred to the queen's marriage and predicted that serious consequences would follow if she married a papist.

This bold speech offended men of both parties. Some who had been friendly with Knox now shunned him. Flatterers hurried to report to the queen that Knox had preached against her marriage. Incensed, she ordered him to come to her.

She cried out, "I have borne with you in your severe speaking against me and have sought your favor in every way possible. I have listened to you whenever it pleased you to admonish me. I vow to God I shall be revenged."

Knox waited patiently until her storm of tears subsided before answering. "It is true your Grace and I have had many arguments, though I did not know your Grace was offended at me. When it shall please God to deliver you from the bondage of darkness and error in which you have been nourished for the lack of true doctrine, then my words will not be offensive. Few are offended at what I say except when I preach. And there, Madam, I am not master of myself, but must obey Him who commands me to speak plainly and to flatter no flesh upon the face of the earth."

"But what have you to do with my marriage?"

"If it please your Majesty patiently to hear me, I shall speak the truth in plain words. I am sent to preach the gospel of Jesus Christ, and it has two parts, repentance and faith. Now, Madam, in preaching repentance, it is necessary to tell men their sins so that they may know where they offend. Most of your nobility are so eager for your good will, that neither God's Word nor the good of the commonwealth are rightly regarded. Therefore, I must speak so that they may know their duty."

"But what have you to do with my marriage? And what are you in this commonwealth?"

"I am a subject born within the realm, Madam. Although I am not an earl or a lord, yet God has made me a profitable servant, however low I may be in your eyes. I am obligated to warn of such things that may hurt the commonwealth no less than the nobles, for both my vocation and my conscience demand plain speech. Therefore I say to you, Madam, what I said in public. If the nobles of this land consent that you be subject to an infidel husband, they do renounce Christ and banish His truth from them; they betray the freedom of this realm; and in the end they shall hurt you."

The queen was furious and burst into angry tears. Knox waited while those standing near tried to check the inordinate passion.

Finally he said, "I never delighted in the weeping of any of God's creatures. I can scarcely abide the tears of my own boys whom my hand corrects, much less can I rejoice in your Majesty's weeping. Seeing that I have given you no reason to be offended, but have spoken the truth as my vocation demands of me, I must endure your Majesty's tears rather than hurt my conscience or betray my commonwealth through my silence."

Mary's tears at this time were more of anger than of grief, since she had already gotten all she wished for in concessions from the Protestant lords. Yet her tears gave rise to misplaced sympathy on the part of some historians. In reality, Mary was furious because one man, and he the most prominent of her subjects, refused to sell his conscience by endorsing her actions. Knox had looked into the future with far-seeing eye and was unable to compromise ignobly when he saw the dangers looming before his country.

At this juncture a woman in Edinburgh

brought a slanderous charge against Knox's moral character. When questioned by the General Assembly, the woman denied having made the accusation. After the Reformer's death, the slander was whispered about, even though there was no basis to it.

However, the queen was determined to get Knox in her power in some way. Finally she believed she had caught him in an offense that required punishment.

The circumstances involved the queen's servants' observing mass in her absence. A number of Protestants, hearing about it, gathered to see if it were true. The servants sent word to the authorities that their lives were in danger. Though there was no evidence of a riot, the queen seized on the incident and ordered two Protestants to be held for trial on the charge of rioting. The Protestants in Edinburgh then asked Knox to write a letter to other Reformed leaders, explaining the problem and asking them to attend the trial. A copy of the letter reached the queen, who sent it to her Privy Council, who declared that the call for others to attend the trial was a treasonable act. Mary had hoped for that and ordered Knox to appear before the council.

Many friends tried to persuade Knox to admit that he was wrong and throw himself on the queen's mercy. This he absolutely refused to do. One close friend even threatened him with the loss of his friendship if he did not submit to the queen, saying that people would not be as patient with him as they had been.

Knox replied that he did not understand such talk. He had only opposed the queen in religious matters; surely no one expected him to bow to her in that. If God stood by him—which He would as long as he trusted Him and preferred His glory rather than his own—he did not care what men thought of him. Furthermore, he did not know what they had "borne" with him about except for hearing him preach the Word. He would be sorry if they rejected that, but they would be the ones to suffer.

When pressure was still applied to get him to submit to the queen to ward off her resentment, he replied, "I cannot confess a fault where there is none. I have not learned to cry treason at everything which the multitude calls treason, nor to fear what they fear."

The case went to trial, and Knox was called before the queen and the Privy Council one evening in the middle of December. Hearing that Knox had been summoned before the queen, such a crowd of Reformers followed that they filled the room and all the stairs as far as the room where the queen and the council sat.

When the trial began, the queen was seated with faithful assistants on each side who whispered in her ear from time to time.

She looked at Knox and then said to those around, "This man has made me weep and yet never wept a tear himself. I will see if I can cause him to weep."

Secretary Lethington addressed Knox. "The queen's Majesty is informed that you have worked to raise a tumult of her subjects against her. In proof, here is your own letter written in your name. Because her Grace will do nothing without careful advice, she has called you before the nobles who will act as witnesses between you and her."

"Let him acknowledge his handwriting," the queen interrupted. "Then we shall judge the letter's contents."

"I gladly acknowledge this as my handwriting," Knox answered. "I dictated the letter in October to brethren in various places about matters that displeased me. I have confidence that the scribes would not have changed the original nor omitted anything. I acknowledge the handwriting and the contents."

"Read the letter aloud," the queen ordered. "Then answer what I ask of you."

When the letter was read, the queen looked around. "Have you ever heard a more despiteful and treasonable letter, my lords?" she demanded.

When no one answered, Secretary Lethington asked, "Master Knox, are you not sorry from your heart and repentant that the letter passed your pen, and has come to the knowledge of others?"

"My lord, before I repent, I must know my offense."

"Offense!" repeated the secretary. "If there were no more than the calling together of the queen's subjects, the offense cannot be denied."

Knox answered, "If I am guilty in this, I have offended often since I last came to Scotland. For what convocation of the brethren has there ever been that was not brought about by my pen? And no man before has laid it to my charge as a crime."

"Then was then," said Lethington, "and now is now. We have no need of such convocations as we once had."

Knox replied, "There is a difference between a lawful and an unlawful convocation. And I see the poor flock now in as great a danger as ever except that the devil has a mask on his face. Before, he came in with his own face, discovered by open tyranny, seeking the destruction of all who refused idolatry. Then the brethren lawfully gathered to defend their lives. Now the devil comes under the cloak of justice to do what God would not let him do by armed force."

"What is this?" demanded the queen. "Who gave him authority to bring together a convocation of my subjects? Is that not treason?"

"No, Madam. He makes convocation of the people to hear prayers and sermons almost daily," answered one of the lords boldly. "Whatever your Grace think of that, it is not treason."

"Hold your peace," she blazed. "Let him answer for himself." She looked at Knox. "I will say nothing against your religion nor against your meeting for your sermons. But what authority have you to gather my subjects whenever you wish without my orders?"

"Madam, I have never convened four persons in Scotland except at the order of the brethren. I have given many advertisements, and great multitudes have gathered. If your Grace complains that this has been done without your Grace's commandment, I answer that so has all that God has blessed within this realm. I must be convicted by a just law that I have done wrong in writing this letter before I can be sorry or repent for doing it as many would persuade me. I wrote at the direction of the General Assembly of this realm, and therefore I think that I have done no wrong."

"You shall not escape so easily," stormed the queen. "Is it not treason, my lords, to accuse a prince of cruelty? I think there are laws of Parliament against such whisperers. This part of your own letter reads, 'These dreadful summons is directed against them (the two Protestants who have been arrested) to open a door to execute cruelty upon a greater multitude.' Now, what do you answer to that?"

Knox replied, "Is it lawful for me to answer, or shall I be condemned before I be heard? I will first ask a question of your Grace and of this most honorable audience. Does your Grace not know that the obstinate papists are deadly enemies to all those who profess the gospel of Jesus Christ, and that they desire to exterminate them and the true doctrines taught within this realm?"

The queen said nothing, but all the lords together exclaimed, "God forbid that the papists have power over the lives of the people or the doctrines. Experience has taught us what cruelty lies in their hearts."

Knox continued, "All will grant, then, that it would be a barbarous cruelty to destroy the multitude within this realm who profess the gospel. Yet they have often attempted to do so by force as actions of late prove. Since God in His providence has prevented them from doing so, they have conceived more crafty and dangerous practices, namely, to make the prince do something under pretense of the law. What they could not do by naked force, they will perform by crafty design. Do you think, my lords, that the insatiable cruelty of the papists within this realm will end with the murder of the two brethren who have been unjustly summoned and accused? By condemning these two, they intend to prepare the way for a bloody enterprise against all."

He looked at Mary. "I do not in my letter

accuse your Grace of a cruel nature. But I affirm yet again that the pestilent papists who have inflamed your Grace without cause against these poor men here, are the sons of the devil. Therefore they must obey the desires of their father who has been a liar and a murderer from the beginning."

Someone sneered, "You forget that you are not in the pulpit."

Knox thundered, "I am in the place where conscience demands that I speak the truth, and therefore the truth I speak. And I must add, Madam, that honest, gentle, and meek natures may be altered by wicked and corrupt counselors. We have an example in Nero, who listened to flatterers. History testifies to the enormity of his crimes. Now I speak plainly, Madam. Papists and enemies of Jesus Christ have your Grace's ear at all times. I assure your Grace they are dangerous counselors, as your mother found."

At this, Secretary Lethington whispered something to the queen. She looked at Knox. "You speak smoothly here before my lords. But the last time that I spoke with you secretly, you caused me to weep many salt tears, and said stubbornly that you cared nothing for my greeting."

Knox replied, "This is the second time your Grace has burdened me with that crime. And I must answer lest my silence prove my guilt. Your Grace charged me that I had irreverently handled you in the pulpit.

When I denied it, you asked what business your marriage was to me that I should meddle in it. I replied that I was a worm of the earth, and yet a subject of this commonwealth. But as a minister whom God had called, I was a watchman both over the realm and over the church of God within the realm. For that reason I was in conscience bound to blow the trumpet publicly whenever I saw danger either to the realm or to the church.

"But when a marriage was planned between your Grace and the Spanish ally, I said that, unless the nobles made sure that neither you nor your husband hurt this realm or the poor church of God in it, I would pronounce them traitors to the commonwealth and enemies of God and His truth. At these words your Grace burst forth into uncontrollable weeping. When nothing stopped your tears, I said I had no pleasure in seeing any creature weep, not even my own children when I had punished them. But I said I must suffer your displeasure, for if I do not speak the truth, I betray both the church and the commonwealth."

The secretary conferred with the queen and then dismissed Knox. Before leaving he said, "Madam, I pray God to purge your heart from Catholicism and to preserve you from the counsel of flatterers. Experience has shown to what straits false counsellors have brought famous princes."

After Knox left, the queen retired with her cabinet so that the vote could be taken to decide if Knox had offended her Majesty. The nobles voted unanimously that they could find no offense in his actions. When the queen returned and heard the result, she commanded the nobles to vote again. They were incensed at the order, demanding, "Shall the presence of a woman make us offend God and condemn an innocent person against our conscience for the pleasure of anyone?"

All the nobles agreed in absolving Knox, praising his modesty and his sensible answers. Among all the flatterers in the court, none dared accuse him. God ruled their tongues as He had once ruled the tongue of Balaam when he tried to curse God's people (Numbers 23). When the queen began to upbraid one of the nobles, he replied coldly, "Your Grace should remember that it was not liking for the man or love of his doctrines that moved me to absolve him. It was the simple truth he stated that moved me."

That night there was no dancing and music in the court, for the queen was disappointed in her purpose. She had planned to have John Knox in her power legally by vote of the nobles, and was deeply angry that her adversary had escaped her so triumphantly.

To appease her anger, Lord Murray and other nobles still urged him to confess to an offense and be forgiven. They insisted his only punishment would be a brief imprisonment in the castle of Edinburgh and then immediate release.

"God forbid," he said, "that by confessing I should condemn those noble men who risked the displeasure of the queen by voting their conscience. I can never confess to being a mover of sedition."

Knox took no part in the General Assembly meetings later that month. But when the business was finished, he reported the summons before the queen and asked the church to pass judgment on the matter. If it did not either absolve or condemn him, he would never again open his mouth to preach or speak. The assembly justified him, saying that he had acted not for himself but for them all.

Knox remarried in March 1564, having been a widower for more than three years. His new wife, Margaret Stewart, was a daughter of Lord Ochiltree, a staunch partisan of Knox. Because the Ochiltree family had royal blood, Roman Catholic writers claimed the marriage was proof of Knox's great ambition and of his desire to have his children sit on the throne.

Although Scotland seemed quiet during 1564, the Catholics were uniting with Mary to curb the freedom of the pulpit. They won over some of the more timid Reformers and tried to get the approval of leading members of the General Assembly to their views.

They were aiming chiefly to quiet Knox, of course.

He knew it was essential that the Reformed ministers be able to speak freely in the presence of a corrupt court and the scheming priesthood. Knox and Secretary Maitland debated the subject at a conference of leading statesmen and ministers of the church. Knox defended the main points of his doctrine that had offended the court. Both men were skilled in debate, and each presented his arguments in keeping with his character.

At the end of the debate, Secretary Maitland insisted that the conference members should vote on the question. He wanted them to establish uniformity of doctrine among the ministers. Knox vigorously protested the motion on the grounds that the General Assembly had agreed to attend the meeting only on condition that nothing be brought to a vote. The conference leaders finally decided that the opinions of those present would be taken but would not be binding.

John Craig, Knox's assistant, spoke for the Reformed side. He reminded the conference that when laws contrary to the laws of God and the true principles of government were put into effect through the negligence of the people or by the tyranny of rulers, the people or their posterity had a right to demand that such laws be reformed.

Craig's speech alarmed the courtiers, fearing it might influence the opinions of others. Knox was asked to write Calvin to get his opinion on the subject. Knox refused, saying that he had previously asked the advice of eminent foreign clergy on this question of the relations between a ruler and his subjects. If he asked again, they would accuse him of forgetfulness or of inconsistency. He suggested that someone else write Calvin about the doctrines just now discussed and ask his opinion of them. Though all thought the suggestion reasonable, no one would volunteer to do so. The conference broke up without any action's being taken.

Another Parliament met in December 1564, but again nothing was done to make the Protestant religion secure in Scotland, because the queen's marriage had been the all-absorbing topic. Mary's ministers had been anxiously negotiating a marriage for some time with both the English and foreign courts. Then suddenly the strong passion she felt for Lord Darnley introduced a disturbing element into the marriage question. Such a union was distasteful to the people in the nation, because Darnley was inclined to Catholicism. With both queen and consort as Catholics, Protestant problems would increase.

The nobles who were determined to have a settlement favoring the Protestants, gave their consent to the marriage only if the Protestant faith was legally established in the country. The queen agreed to summon a Parliament for this purpose, but then delayed its meeting on a trumped-up excuse. She succeeded, by favors and promises, in gaining the support of enough nobles to allow her marriage to Darnley in July 1565. She then moved swiftly to proclaim her husband king without the consent of the estates of the realm.

Darnley's vain and vindictive behavior added to the unrest over the marriage. He immediately overthrew Lord Murray's wise influence in court and put in power those favorable to him. In addition, David Rizzio, a low-bred Italian, wormed himself into Mary's confidence. Lord Murray was declared an outlaw, while Lord Bothwell and others who were antagonistic to the Reformed doctrines and interested only in their own advancement, returned to power in the court.

The dissatisfied lords, still loyal to the queen, tried to reconcile differences with her. They agreed to submit their cause to be lawfully tried. When Mary refused to listen and marched against them with an army, they fled to England for protection under Queen Elizabeth. The horizon of Protestantism in Scotland darkened ominously.

7

For a while Mary pretended to treat
Protestants leniently, even saying she was
willing to listen to their sermons, especially
by those who were "mild and sweet-
natured." But this was only a brief respite,
and the queen soon stated flatly that she
would never leave the religion in which she
had been nourished and brought up.

She was still on hostile terms with Knox
and would like to have proved him an
accomplice in an insurrection led by Lord
Murray. But Knox had kept himself clear
of that action, though his father-in-law
had joined it. Mary soon found another
excuse to accuse Knox.

Darnley attended the service in Saint
Giles's Church in August, sitting on a throne
that had been prepared for him. In his
sermon for the day, Knox quoted the
Scripture, "I will give children to be their

princes, and babes shall rule over them . . . children are their oppressors, and women rule over them" (Isaiah 3:4, 12). He reminded the congregation that God had punished Ahab for not correcting his idolatrous wife Jezebel.

Even though Knox did not apply the passage to the king and queen, Darnley was furious. When he returned to the palace, he refused to eat and bitterly complained to the queen. Knox was taken before the Privy Council, accused of offending the king, and ordered not to preach as long as their Majesties were in Edinburgh.

Knox replied, "I have spoken nothing but according to the text. If the church should command me either to speak or to abstain, I would obey so far as the Word of God would permit me." He not only stood by what he had said in the pulpit, but added, "As the king, for the queen's pleasure, has gone to mass and dishonored the Lord God, so should He in His justice, make her the instrument of his overthrow."

Enraged at this answer, the queen burst into tears. The court left Edinburgh, but later, returning, the queen did not stop Knox from preaching because of popular sympathy for him. He continued to preach as boldly as formerly.

The General Assembly then commissioned Knox to visit churches in the south of Scotland and to write encouraging letters to the ministers, exhorters, and readers throughout the kingdom. Many were threatening to give up their positions because they were not being paid. Knox wrote to encourage them to continue in their duties. He also encouraged the people to help relieve the financial need of those who ministered among them.

The General Assembly had ordered a general fast because of the dangers facing the whole Protestant cause and asked Knox to write a treatise on fasting. This concern of the General Assembly was justified as the queen renewed her efforts to restore Catholicism in Scotland. Darnley openly admitted that he was a Catholic, and some of the nobles followed his example. Murray and other leading Protestants were ordered to appear before Parliament in March 1566. The Lords of the Articles were the queen's choices, and Catholic clergy were reinstated in Parliament.

Suddenly Rizzio, the queen's favorite, was murdered, upsetting the entire political situation. Darnley had become jealous of him and entered into a secret conspiracy with some of the Protestant nobles to murder Rizzio. As a result, the Catholic counselors fled the court, the Protestant nobles in exile in England returned, and Parliament was dissolved without accomplishing Mary's purpose of stamping out Protestantism.

The queen easily persuaded the weak king to disown the act that he had instigated and to retire with her to Dunbar. His weak, cowardly conduct brought contempt from the people, and did not reinstate him in Mary's affections.

In all this upheaval, Knox was still aware of how strong the queen's animosity was toward him. He left Edinburgh for semi-retirement in Kyle, where he wrote a large part of his *History*. Early in 1567 he visited England to see his two sons. While he was in England, Darnley was assassinated, once again changing events in Scotland.

Since Rizzio's murder, Mary had hated her husband. Even the birth of their son, James VI, did not reconcile them. In the meantime, the violent earl of Bothwell had gained the queen's affections. While living in Glasgow, Darnley became violently ill. Mary visited him and urged him to return to Edinburgh. He was taken to a small house near the city walls. On the night of February 10, 1567, the house was blown apart by gunpowder. Darnley's body was found in the garden, and it was reported that he had been strangled. Aroused public feeling clamored that Bothwell was the murderer and the queen his accomplice.

Bothwell was brought to trial, which proved to be a farce, for the queen had him cleared, and then rewarded him with large tracts of land. He then kidnapped

Mary, probably with her connivance, got a divorce from his wife, and married the queen in May. Knox's colleague, Craig, refused to publish the banns of the adulterous marriage, and boldly condemned it, even though many of the Scottish lords accepted it silently.

However, shortly, discontented lords gathered their forces, compelling Bothwell to flee and Mary to surrender to them. She was taken to Lochleven Castle and compelled to sign a deed of abdication. It was a bitter blow to her to have to appoint Lord Murray as regent of the kingdom while her son was an infant.

Knox had returned to Edinburgh about the time the queen had fled with Bothwell. In July 1567, he preached a sermon at the coronation of James VI in the church in Stirling. Knox agreed with those who insisted that the deposed queen ought to be brought to trial and put to death if she were found guilty of the death of her husband and of an adulterous union with Bothwell. They insisted that murder and adultery were crimes for which all must be punished, no matter how high their station in life.

Though Knox eventually acquiesced in the decision to keep the queen in prison, his personal views did not change. Later, when civil war resulted from her escape from prison, he insisted that the nation was suffering for its criminal leniency toward her.

Lord Murray was formally invested with the regency in August 1567. He immediately began efforts to secure the peace of the kingdom and settle church affairs. Calling Parliament to meet in December, Murray and the Privy Council chose representatives to meet beforehand and decide which matters to bring before Parliament. Knox and four other ministers were selected to confer on matters pertaining to the church.

Knox preached at the opening of the Parliament, urging it to settle religious matters first and then other business would be settled successfully. Parliament responded and ratified all the acts which had been passed in 1560, favoring the Protestant religion and adding new statutes. These provided that no prince could have authority in the kingdom unless he took an oath to maintain the Protestant religion. Furthermore, only Protestants should hold any office except for those positions that were hereditary or already held for life. Various other statutes were enacted, including a better system of paying the ministers' salaries and supporting education.

Knox was appointed to a committee to draw up the particular points that pertained to ecclesiastical affairs to present to the next meeting of Parliament. The General Assembly also commissioned him to act for it and to represent its interests before the regent.

Murray's government was wise and peaceful. During his brief rule the country was at rest because the church and the court were not feuding. Whenever it was in his power, he complied with the petitions of the General Assembly. The financial difficulties between church and court were at last settled amicably.

With his goal attained of seeing Protestantism safely established in Scotland, Knox hoped to be free from public affairs. He was not well and wanted to have time to meditate and prepare for death, which he felt was rapidly encroaching.

Unfortunately, his trials were not over. Once again he saw the security of the Reformed religion threatened and the country involved in civil war. The regent was not only opposed by Catholics, but Protestant lords were alienated because of their personal and family quarrels. Others were hostile to Murray for various reasons. He managed to crush two revolts and caused Mary to flee to England. Then the Catholics hired assassins to kill him, and several attempts were made. Finally in 1568 the archbishop of Saint Andrews was involved through his nephew in a plot that was successful.

The country was in deep shock and dismay at Murray's death and demanded vengeance. The actual murderer got safely out of the country, and the others involved claimed innocence when they saw the anger of the people.

Knox was overwhelmed at Murray's death, for they had been close friends in earlier years. Even after the strain in their relationship, Knox continued to have confidence in Murray's religious beliefs and had admired his ability in government. Knox considered the regent's death a severe blow to the country and the forerunner of other evils.

In his sermon lamenting Murray, he said, "Surely God in His great mercy raised up pious rulers, and took them away in His displeasure on account of the sins of the nation. He is at rest, O Lord, but we are left in extreme misery."

To minimize the effects of Murray's death, a false account circulated that Murray and Knox and others intended to set aside the young king and crown Murray in his place. The charge was fabricated by Thomas Maitland, the secretary's brother, but was easily discredited.

Knox preached a sermon before Murray's funeral on the words, "Blessed are the dead which die in the Lord." As he praised Murray and mourned his loss, the three thousand people at the service dissolved in tears.

Knox's own grief further shattered his

health, and a stroke in October affected his speech. His enemies rejoiced and spread the rumor that he was dead. No life in the nation was as closely watched as his by both friends and foes.

8

Knox partially regained his health so that, as his speech returned, he was able to preach on Sundays. He was needed; the times were once again dark and lowering. The earl of Lennox, appointed as regent, was a weak substitute for Murray, and the queen's party soon came back to power. A bitter personal blow to Knox came from the defection of Lord Kirkcaldy from the Protestant cause. Kirkcaldy was governor of the Castle of Edinburgh, and he surrendered that famous stronghold to the queen's forces. Kirkcaldy's defection and a personal quarrel between him and Knox made matters critical.

Knox had not been afraid to reprove a queen and now did not hesitate to criticize Kirkcaldy from the pulpit. Threats and counterthreats flew between the followers of each. Slanderous complaints of sedition and railing against the queen were made against Knox. The General Assembly commanded the anonymous accusers to prove their charges at a meeting in March 1571. When they did not do so, Knox refuted the slander from his pulpit in Saint Giles'. He admitted that he had boldly called wickedness by its own terms.

As to the charge that he did not pray for the queen, he replied, "I am not bound to pray for her in this place, for she is not a sovereign to me. I am not a man of law that has my tongue to sell for silver or the favor of the world."

Knox insisted that he lived in obedience to the lawful authority of the estates which had deposed the queen, and he prayed that God would confound the aims of the Catholics. He was accustomed to threats against his life, he said, and had reached an age at which he was not apt to flee very far. Even though his contemporaries might not know how he had worked for his country, future ages would be compelled to understand. He dared his enemies to meet him face-to-face, by saying, "It seems unreasonable that, in my decrepit age, I shall be compelled to fight against shadows and owlets that dare not abide the light."

Knox never went out now except on Sunday to preach in the morning service.

He was so feeble that he was not able to climb into the pulpit without assistance. In March 1570, he had written his friend, Sir William Douglas, the laird of Lochleven, that he had taken his "goodnight of the world. Yet, whenever I see the church and the commonwealth seriously in danger, I forget my infirmities and mingle in the conflict."

In April 1571, his living situation in Edinburgh became critical after Kirkcaldy allowed forces into the castle who were favorable to the queen. His friends urged him to leave the city because of threats and an actual attempt on his life, but he refused. His friends finally persuaded him to leave by insisting that if he were attacked, they would risk their lives in his defense, and he would be responsible if blood were shed. Against his will, he left the city and traveled slowly to Saint Andrews. Many of his friends were also driven from Edinburgh. For a time the church of Edinburgh was dissolved and the celebration of the Lord's Supper suspended. Instead of singing and preaching, nothing was heard but the firing of cannons.

Petty skirmishes and disgraceful acts of retaliation occurred daily and the Protestants were harassed constantly. A man was attacked and mutilated simply because his name was Knox, proof of the danger the Reformer would have been in had he remained in the city. Even in Saint Andrews he was verbally attacked. His denunciations of the murders of Darnley and Regent Murray stirred opposition. Robert Hamilton, a minister in the city, spread the rumor that Knox had been part of the plot to kill Darnley. When challenged by Knox, he denied spreading the rumor. Then Hamilton's brother, a professor at the university, accused Knox to the university authorities of intolerable railing in his sermons. Knox successfully defended himself to the university professors, at the same time reminding them that he came before them voluntarily. His appearance did not take away the liberty of the pulpit nor the authority of the regular church courts. The judgment of religious doctrines belonged to the church, not to any university.

Two important events occurred that affected the destiny of the Scottish Protestant church. Dumbarton Castle was seized by the regent's forces in April 1571. Archbishop Hamilton was captured, tried, condemned, and hanged. Among his many crimes, he confessed that he was involved in Regent Murray's murder. Then, in September, Stirling was seized and Regent Lennox was killed in revenge for the death of the archbishop.

The earl of Mar became regent and conscientiously worked to restore peace to the kingdom. An important question arose again concerning church revenues. Because of the influence of the earl of Morton, the income from bishoprics was being given to certain ministers who in turn gave it to the noblemen who had obtained favors for them from the court. The affair made a great stir, and the General Assembly protested the practice at the next meeting of Parliament.

However, Parliament confirmed this new scheme for seizing church properties and revenues. Bishoprics and other honors were openly conferred on noblemen, on persons totally unqualified for the ministry, and even on minors. This was the origin of the Episcopal system that was brought into the Reformed church of Scotland while James VI was a minor. The General Assembly took a stand on the issue and in a formal resolution repudiated the retention of all titles such as archbishop, bishop, and so on, which reflected Catholicism.

Knox had always denounced these encroachments on the rights and property of the church. He believed that power could be delegated in certain circumstances to ministers to inspect congregations. He had recommended the appointment of superintendents when the Reformed churches were first established in Scotland. But he did not believe that any class of office holders in the church, no matter what the name, was superior to ministers. It was a view he had consistently held. He had written a friend several years earlier, "I would most gladly pass through the course that God has appointed me, giving thanks to His holy name, for it has pleased His mercy to make me, not a lord bishop, but a painful preacher of His blessed gospel."

In previous correspondence with a friend he had described the government of the Scottish church, stressing that no titles were used. Now the friend answered, congratulating Knox that he had banished the order of bishops and warning him not to let titles reenter under the deceitful pretext of maintaining unity. Unfortunately, the warning came too late.

Knox publicly stated his views on the subject when the archbishop of Saint Andrews was installed. Knox preached the sermon as usual, and then the earl of Morton, who was largely responsible for bringing in the titles, asked him to inaugurate the archbishop. Knox adamantly refused, denouncing both the donor and the recipient of the bishopric. Knox was accused of refusing because he was disappointed that he had not been granted the office of archbishop. He replied that he had to speak out against the bestowing of a bishopric in keeping with his conscience. He reminded his critics that a different order had been settled for the Church of Scotland in the

Book of Discipline, which had been subscribed to by the nobles and ratified by Parliament. In the General Assembly meeting the following month he again protested both the election of the archbishop of Saint Andrews and the making of bishops.

Although Knox's health was obviously declining, he shook off his weakness when he was in the pulpit and electrified the audience with his eloquence.

A student at Saint Andrews wrote of Knox's appearance before the students in 1571. "Of all the benefits that I had that year was the coming of that most notable prophet and apostle of our nation, Mr. John Knox, to Saint Andrews. . . . I heard him teach there the prophecies of Daniel that summer and the winter following. In the opening of his text, he was moderate the space of an half hour. But when he entered to application, he made me so to thrill and tremble, that I could not hold a pen to write. He was very weak . . . and was lifted up to the pulpit where he behooved to lean at his first entry. But, ere he had done with his sermon, he was so active and vigorous, that he was like to beat the pulpit in pieces and fly out of it."

Knox spent much of his time in Saint Andrews encouraging the students. He also wrote and published a vindication of the Reformed religion in answer to a letter from a Scottish Jesuit. He published this work as a farewell address to the world and as a dying testimony to the truth he had so long taught and defended. Along with it he published one of the letters he had written to his mother-in-law, who had just died. He now frequently confessed that he was "weary of the world" and "thirsting to depart."

In August 1572 he wrote a touching letter of farewell to the General Assembly. From this time on, his health failed so rapidly that it seemed he would end his days at Saint Andrews. However, his old congregation at Saint Giles's wanted to hear him once more before he died. They begged him to come to Edinburgh if his health would permit. He agreed to return on the understanding that he would not keep still about the conduct of those who held the Castle of Edinburgh, "whose treasonable and tyrannical deeds I will cry out against as long as I am able to speak."

He arrived in Edinburgh in September. There his heart was torn with anguish at the news from France of the Saint Bartholomew massacre, a terrible crime for which the pope ordered thanksgiving in Rome. Knox thundered God's vengeance against that "cruel murderer and false traitor, the king of France."

Knox's last public appearance was the ninth of November, when he presided at the installation of his successor at Saint

Giles's Church. After pronouncing the benediction, he was taken home and never came out again alive.

He began to fail perceptibly and was unable to read his customary Scripture. Either his wife or his secretary read regularly to him from John 17, Isaiah 53, and a chapter from Ephesians. He sometimes asked for certain psalms and for Calvin's French sermons on Ephesians. Occasionally he seemed to be asleep, but when asked, he replied, "I hear, praise God, and understand far better."

On his deathbed, he seemed almost to have the gift of prophetic insight as he talked with those standing near. He sent urgent messages to Kirkcaldy, his former ally in the Reformed faith, begging him to repent or else he would be "disgracefully dragged from his nest to punishment and hung on a gallows before the face of the sun, unless he speedily amend his life and flee to the mercy of God." He told those near him, "That man's soul is dear to me, and I would not have it perish if I could save it."

Receiving Kirkcaldy's contemptuous response, Knox grieved for him, trusting that "his soul would be saved, though his body would come to a miserable end."

He continued to receive many visitors of every rank, though he had great difficulty breathing and spoke only with pain. All who came to him received loving counsel suited to their needs. He urged the earl of Morton to use the riches, wisdom, and friends God had given him for God's glory, the furthering of the gospel, the maintenance of the church of God, and then for the welfare of the king and his realm and subjects. "If you do so, God shall bless you and honor you. But if you do it not, God shall spoil you of these benefits, and your end shall be ignominy and shame."

On Friday, November 21, he ordered his casket made. During that day he spent much time in meditation and prayer. Listeners heard him say, "Come, Lord Jesus; into Thy hand I commend my spirit. Be merciful, Lord, to Thy church, which Thou hast redeemed. Give peace to this afflicted commonwealth. Raise up faithful pastors who will take charge of Thy church. Grant us, Lord, the perfect hatred of sin, both by the evidences of Thy wrath and mercy."

He often spoke to those who stood by, saying, "Oh serve the Lord in fear, and death shall not be terrible to you. Nay, blessed shall death be to those who have felt the power of the death of the only begotten Son of God."

On Sunday the twenty-third, the first day of the national fast, he suddenly exclaimed, "If any be present, let them come and see the work of God." After a moment he exclaimed again, "I have been these last two nights in meditation on the troubled state of the church of God, the spouse of Jesus Christ, despised of the world, but precious in the sight of God. I have been called to God for her, and have committed her to her head, Jesus Christ. I have fought against spiritual wickedness in heavenly things, and have prevailed. I have been in heaven and have possession. I have tasted of the heavenly joys where presently I will be."

When someone asked if he felt much pain, he answered that he was willing to lie there for years if God so pleased. He slept very little, but was constantly active in meditation and prayer and exhortation.

"Lord, grant true pastors to Thy church that purity of doctrine may be retained. Restore peace again to this commonwealth with godly rulers and magistrates." Then, stretching his hands toward heaven he said, "Lord, I commend my spirit, soul, and body, and all into Thy hands. Thou knowest, O Lord, my troubles; I do not murmur against Thee."

His exclamations were so frequent that those standing near could not remember all that he said. He was only silent when someone was reading or praying.

Monday, November 24, was his last day on earth. That morning he insisted on getting up. He sat in a chair for about half an hour and then was put to bed. As the day went on, it was clear that the end was near. His wife and three of his closest friends took turns sitting beside him. One asked if he had any pain.

He answered, "It is no painful pain, but such a pain as shall soon, I trust, put an end to the battle. I must leave the care of my wife and children to you, to whom you must be a husband in my place."

About three in the afternoon he asked his wife to read First Corinthians 15 to him. "Oh what sweet consolation the Lord has given me from that chapter," he said, when she finished. Then he asked her to read the seventeenth chapter of John and a part of Calvin's sermons on Ephesians.

After this he seemed to fall into a deep sleep, interrupted by heavy moans. When he awakened, he was asked the reason for the deep sighs. He answered, "I have often during my frail life sustained many assaults from Satan. But now he has assailed me most fearfully, and put forth all his strength to devour and make an end of me at once.

"Often before he has placed my sins before my eyes, often tempted me to despair, often endeavored to ensnare me by the allurements of the world. But these weapons were broken by the sword of the Spirit, the Word of God, and the enemy failed. Now he has attacked me in another way. The cunning serpent has tried to persuade me that I have merited heaven and eternal blessedness by the faithful discharge of my ministry. But blessed be God, who has enabled me to beat down and quench this fiery dart, by suggesting to me such Scripture as 'What hast thou that thou hast not received?' and 'By the grace of God I am what I am. Not I but the grace of God in me.' Upon this, as one vanquished, he left me.

"Wherefore, I gave thanks to my God through Jesus Christ who has been pleased to give me the victory. I am persuaded that the tempter shall not again attack me, but, within a short time, I shall, without any great pain of body or anguish of mind, exchange this mortal and miserable life for a blessed immortality through Jesus Christ."

He then lay quiet for some hours. When asked if he had heard those with him reading the evening prayers, he replied, "Would to God that you and all men had heard them as I have heard them. I praise God for that heavenly sound." Then he gave a deep sigh and said, "Now it is come."

His friends realized that he could not speak and asked him to give them a sign that he heard them and died in peace. In answer, he lifted one of his hands.

Knox was only sixty-seven when he died, but in that time he had lived more than many men. His career had been distinguished both for its extraordinary labors and for its equally extraordinary cares and anxieties. Probably few men passed through so many dangers and yet lived to finish the course in peace and honor. Knox was interred in the churchyard of Saint Giles's on November 26, 1572, with great crowds coming to the funeral. Morton, the newly-elected regent, well summed his character in the brief eulogy, "Here lies one who never feared the face of man."

The Reformer was survived by his second wife and her three daughters and by the two sons of his first wife.

An imposing monument to his memory was erected in Glasgow in 1825. Inscriptions on the four sides of the column, which is topped by a large statue of Knox, tell of his life and service.

The inscription on the north side reads,

To testify gratitude for inestimable services in the cause of religion, education, and civil liberty; to awaken admiration of that integrity, disinterestedness, and courage, which stood unshaken in the midst of trials, and in the maintenance of the highest objects; and, finally, to cherish unceasing reverence for the principles and blessings of that great Reformation, by the influence of which our country, through the midst of difficulties, has risen to honor, prosperity, and happiness—this Monument is erected by voluntary contributions, to the memory of John Knox, the chief instrument, under God, of the Reformation of Scotland, on the 22nd day of September, 1825. He died, rejoicing in the faith of the Gospel, at Edinburgh, on the 24th of November, 1572, in the sixty-seventh year of his age.

The great work Knox was called to do could not have been accomplished by a rosewater policy. It required a strong, invincible character such as his. While his supporters were struck with admiration at his powers, the Roman Catholics were equally strong in denouncing him. But his work was deep and permanent. He was a true type of the religious Reformer, dominated by the mighty task that lay before him, and indifferent to everything that hindered its accomplishment. But he was far too broad-minded a man, and possessed too much sterling good sense and ready wit, to be justly described as a fanatic. He was always manly and human in his enthusiasms. He brought about a greater revolution than could have been accomplished by the sword, for he set springs in motion that ultimately transformed the religious ideas and aspirations of the nation.

He had an acute intelligence, was vigorous and bold in his conceptions, and had the stamp of an unmistakable individuality upon everything he did. To a love of study he joined a desire for active employment. His zeal, intrepidity, and independence of mind were the most conspicuous features of his character.

He was incorruptible, as much above the solicitations of his friends as he was undismayed by the threats of his enemies. He was swayed by two lofty principles— love for his country and an all-consuming desire to advance the glory of God. These will keep his memory green, and he will go down for all time as one of the world's true heroes.